endorsed for
Edexcel

Edexcel GCSE (9-1)
History

Superpower relations and the Cold War, 1941–91

Series Editor: Angela Leonard   Authors: Christopher Catherwood   Nigel Kelly

PEARSON

Published by Pearson Education Limited, 80 Strand, London, WC2R 0RL.

www.pearsonschoolsandfecolleges.co.uk

Copies of official specifications for all Edexcel qualifications may be found on the website: www.edexcel.com

Text © Pearson Education Limited 2016

Series editor: Angela Leonard
Designed by Colin Tilley Loughrey, Pearson Education Limited
Typeset by Phoenix Photosetting, Chatham, Kent
Original illustrations © Pearson Education Limited
Illustrated by KJA Artists Illustration Agency and Phoenix Photosetting, Chatham, Kent.

Cover design by Colin Tilley Loughrey
Picture research by Ewout Buckens
Cover photo © Getty Images: Grey Villet / The LIFE Images Collection

The right of Christopher Catherwood and Nigel Kelly to be identified as author of this work has been asserted by her in accordance with the Copyright, Designs and Patents Act 1988.

First published 2016

22 21 20
12 11 10

British Library Cataloguing in Publication Data
A catalogue record for this book is available from the British Library.
ISBN 978 1 292 12727 9

Printed in Slovakia by Neografia

A note from the publisher
In order to ensure that this resource offers high-quality support for the associated Pearson qualification, it has been through a review process by the awarding body. This process confirms that this resource fully covers the teaching and learning content of the specification or part of a specification at which it is aimed. It also confirms that it demonstrates an appropriate balance between the development of subject skills, knowledge and understanding, in addition to preparation for assessment.

Endorsement does not cover any guidance on assessment activities or processes (e.g. practice questions or advice on how to answer assessment questions), included in the resource nor does it prescribe any particular approach to the teaching or delivery of a related course.

While the publishers have made every attempt to ensure that advice on the qualification and its assessment is accurate, the official specification and associated assessment guidance materials are the only authoritative source of information and should always be referred to for definitive guidance.

Pearson examiners have not contributed to any sections in this resource relevant to examination papers for which they have responsibility.

Examiners will not use endorsed resources as a source of material for any assessment set by Pearson.

Endorsement of a resource does not mean that the resource is required to achieve this Pearson qualification, nor does it mean that it is the only suitable material available to support the qualification, and any resource lists produced by the awarding body shall include this and other appropriate resources.

Websites
Pearson Education Limited is not responsible for the content of any external internet sites. It is essential for tutors to preview each website before using it in class so as to ensure that the URL is still accurate, relevant and appropriate. We suggest that tutors bookmark useful websites and consider enabling students to access them through the school/college intranet.

Contents

How to use this book

What's covered?

This book covers the Period Study on Superpower Relations and the Cold War, 1941–91. This unit makes up 20% of your GCSE course, and will be examined in Paper 2.

Period studies cover a specific period of time of around 50 years, and require you to know about and be able to analyse the events surrounding important developments and issues that happened in this period. You need to understand how the different topics covered fit into the overall narrative. This book also explains the different types of exam questions you will need to answer, and includes advice and example answers to help you improve.

Features

As well as a clear, detailed explanation of the key knowledge you will need, you will also find a number of features in the book:

Key terms

Where you see a word followed by an asterisk, like this: Hawks*, you will be able to find a Key Terms box on that page that explains what the word means.

> **Key term**
>
> **Hawks***
>
> During the Cold War, those who supported going to war were known as Hawks. Their counterparts, who tried to find solutions to problems without going to war, were known as Doves.

Activities

Every few pages, you'll find a box containing some activities designed to help check and embed knowledge and get you to really think about what you've studied. The activities start simple, but might get more challenging as you work through them.

Summaries and Checkpoints

At the end of each chunk of learning, the main points are summarised in a series of bullet points – great for embedding the core knowledge, and handy for revision.

Checkpoints help you to check and reflect on your learning. The Strengthen section helps you to consolidate knowledge and understanding, and check that you've grasped the basic ideas and skills.

The Challenge questions push you to go beyond just understanding the information, and into evaluation and analysis of what you've studied.

Sources and Interpretations

Although source work and interpretations do not appear in Paper 2, you'll still find interesting contemporary material throughout the books, showing what people from the period said, thought or created, helping you to build your understanding of people in the past.

> **Source E**
>
> A photograph of children watching as a supply plane arrives in Berlin during the Berlin Airlift.
>
>
>
> **Interpretation 1**
>
> A recent account of the Paris Summit and U-2 incident from the *US Department of State Official History* website.
>
> ```
> Khrushchev had publicly committed himself
> to the idea of "peaceful coexistence" with
> the United States... [Had] the United States
> apologized, he would have continued the summit.
> Eisenhower, however, refused to issue a formal
> apology... . On May 11, Eisenhower finally
> acknowledged his full awareness of the entire
> program and of the Powers flight in particular.
> Moreover, he explained that... such spy
> flights were a necessary element in maintaining
> national defense, and that he planned to
> continue them.
> ```

Extend your knowledge

These features contain useful additional information that adds depth to your knowledge, and to your answers. The information is closely related to the key issues in the unit, and questions are sometimes included, helping you to link the new details to the main content.

> **Extend your knowledge**
>
> **President John F. Kennedy**
>
> John Fitzgerald Kennedy was one of the youngest men ever to be elected President of the United States, he took office aged just 43. Born in 1917, he came from a very wealthy family. He fought in the Second World War and served as a Senator before becoming President. Many, like Khrushchev, saw Kennedy as an inexperienced youth, whose wealth gave him no understanding of the real world. Events in Berlin and Cuba proved Khrushchev's assumptions were wrong.

Exam-style questions and tips

The book also includes extra exam-style questions you can use to practise. These appear in the chapters and are accompanied by a tip to help you get started on an answer.

Exam-style question, Section A

Explain **two** consequences of the Hungarian Uprising in 1956.   **8 marks**

Exam tip

Remember this question is about consequences, not events. So don't spend time saying what happened during the uprising. Focus on explaining what happened as a result of the uprising.

Recap pages

At the end of each chapter, you'll find a page designed to help you to consolidate and reflect on the chapter as a whole. Each recap page includes a recall quiz, ideal for quickly checking your knowledge or for revision. Recap pages also include activities designed to help you summarise and analyse what you've learned, and also reflect on how each chapter links to other parts of the unit.

THINKING HISTORICALLY

These activities are designed to help you develop a better understanding of how history is constructed, and are focused on the key areas of Evidence, Interpretations, Cause & Consequence and Change & Continuity. In the Period Study, you will come across an activity on Cause & Consequence, as this is a key focus for this unit.

The Thinking Historically approach has been developed in conjunction with Dr Arthur Chapman and the Institute of Education, UCL. It is based on research into the misconceptions that can hold students back in history.

THINKING HISTORICALLY > Cause and Consequence (2c) —— conceptual map reference

The Thinking Historically conceptual map can be found at: www.pearsonschools.co.uk/thinkinghistoricallygcse

WRITING HISTORICALLY

At the end of most chapters is a spread dedicated to helping you improve your writing skills. These include simple techniques you can use in your writing to make your answers clearer, more precise and better focused on the question you're answering.

The Writing Historically approach is based on the *Grammar for Writing* pedagogy developed by a team at the University of Exeter and popular in many English departments. Each spread uses examples from the preceding chapter, so it's relevant to what you've just been studying.

Preparing for your exams

At the back of the book, you'll find a special section dedicated to explaining and exemplifying the new Edexcel GCSE History exams. Advice on the demands of this paper, written by Angela Leonard, helps you prepare for and approach the exam with confidence. Each question type is explained through annotated sample answers at two levels, showing clearly how answers can be improved.

Pearson Progression Scale: This icon indicates the Step that a sample answer has been graded at on the Pearson Progression Scale.

This book is also available as an online ActiveBook, which can be licensed for your whole institution.

There is also an ActiveLearn Digital Service available to support delivery of this book, featuring a front-of-class version of the book, lesson plans, worksheets, exam practice PowerPoints, assessments, notes on Thinking Historically and Writing Historically, and more.

ActiveLearn
Digital Service

Timeline: Superpower relations and the Cold War, 1941–91

West

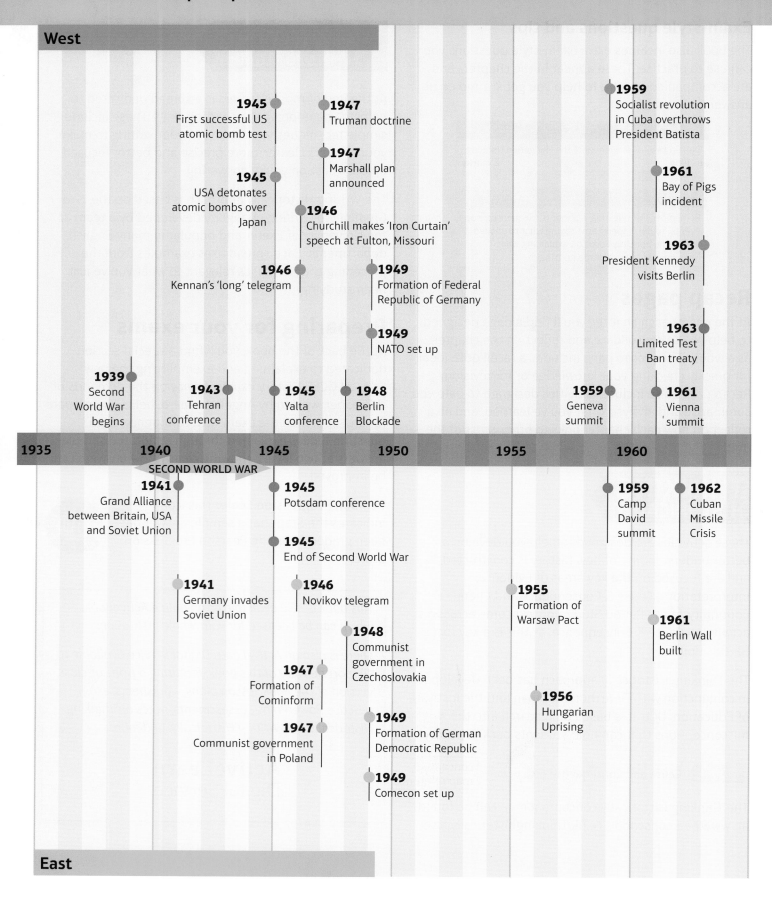

1945
First successful US atomic bomb test

1947
Truman doctrine

1945
USA detonates atomic bombs over Japan

1947
Marshall plan announced

1946
Churchill makes 'Iron Curtain' speech at Fulton, Missouri

1946
Kennan's 'long' telegram

1949
Formation of Federal Republic of Germany

1949
NATO set up

1959
Socialist revolution in Cuba overthrows President Batista

1961
Bay of Pigs incident

1963
President Kennedy visits Berlin

1963
Limited Test Ban treaty

1939
Second World War begins

1943
Tehran conference

1945
Yalta conference

1948
Berlin Blockade

1959
Geneva summit

1961
Vienna summit

| 1935 | 1940 | 1945 | 1950 | 1955 | 1960 |

SECOND WORLD WAR

1941
Grand Alliance between Britain, USA and Soviet Union

1945
Potsdam conference

1959
Camp David summit

1962
Cuban Missile Crisis

1945
End of Second World War

1941
Germany invades Soviet Union

1946
Novikov telegram

1955
Formation of Warsaw Pact

1948
Communist government in Czechoslovakia

1961
Berlin Wall built

1947
Formation of Cominform

1956
Hungarian Uprising

1947
Communist government in Poland

1949
Formation of German Democratic Republic

1949
Comecon set up

East

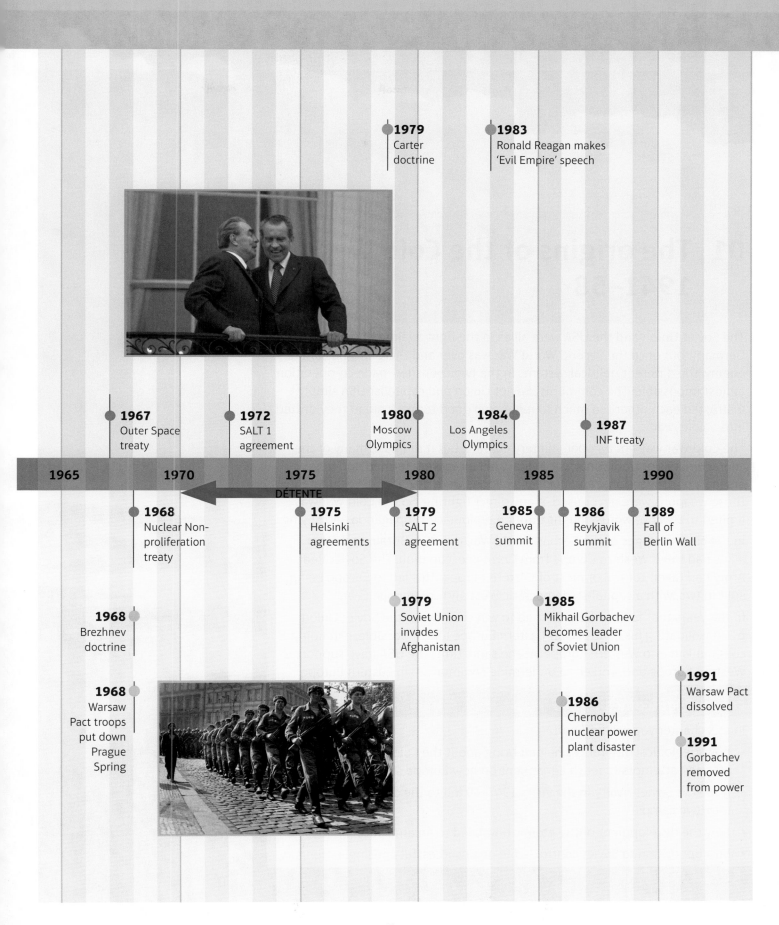

1979
Carter doctrine

1983
Ronald Reagan makes 'Evil Empire' speech

1967
Outer Space treaty

1972
SALT 1 agreement

1980
Moscow Olympics

1984
Los Angeles Olympics

1987
INF treaty

| 1965 | 1970 | 1975 | 1980 | 1985 | 1990 |

DÉTENTE

1968
Nuclear Non-proliferation treaty

1975
Helsinki agreements

1979
SALT 2 agreement

1985
Geneva summit

1986
Reykjavik summit

1989
Fall of Berlin Wall

1968
Brezhnev doctrine

1979
Soviet Union invades Afghanistan

1985
Mikhail Gorbachev becomes leader of Soviet Union

1991
Warsaw Pact dissolved

1968
Warsaw Pact troops put down Prague Spring

1986
Chernobyl nuclear power plant disaster

1991
Gorbachev removed from power

01 | The origins of the Cold War, 1941–58

The Soviet Union and the USA were allies in the fight against Hitler's Germany, but once the Second World War was over and there was no common enemy, the different political systems in the two countries made co-operation almost impossible. The communist Soviet Union and capitalist USA simply distrusted each other too much to remain on good terms. Instead they drifted into a 'cold' war.

The Cold War was not an open military conflict, but it did have many of the characteristics of traditional war. Military alliances were formed and huge arsenals of conventional and nuclear weapons were developed. Fortunately, those weapons were never used in any direct fighting. So the Cold War was limited to a war of words, fought through diplomacy, propaganda and spying.

In the closing stages of the Second World War, the USA, Britain and other allies had freed Western Europe from German occupation. The Soviet Red Army had taken control of most of Eastern Europe. This led to Europe being split in two, with a capitalist, democratic West and communist East.

In the years that followed, Stalin tried to win security for the Soviet Union by consolidating his control over Eastern Europe and, if possible, extending communism into Western Europe. At the same time, the USA gave support to Western Europe and worked to undermine communism in Eastern Europe.

Learning outcomes

In this chapter you will find out:

- how ideological differences helped bring about the Cold War and how they affected attempts to reach agreement on how Europe should be governed
- how US / Soviet rivalry in the years 1947–49 led to the division of Europe into 'two camps'
- how the development of the atomic bomb led to an arms race
- how opposition to Soviet control led to an unsuccessful uprising in Hungary.

1.1 Early tensions between East and West

Learning outcomes

- Know about the political outlooks of the communist Soviet Union and capitalist USA.
- Understand how, as allies during the Second World War, the Soviet Union, the USA and Britain formed plans for the future government of Europe.
- Understand how the alliance turned to rivalry and distrust when the Second World War was over.

During the Second World War, the Soviet Union*, the USA and Britain formed an alliance to fight against Hitler and Nazi Germany. Britain's prime minister, Winston Churchill, nicknamed this alliance 'The Grand Alliance'. As soon as it became clear that Hitler would be defeated, tension and rivalry between the allies began to grow, gradually escalating into the Cold War.

Key term

Soviet Union*

Short for Union of Soviet Socialist Republics (also shortened to USSR). The republics were Russia, Ukraine, Belarus, Kazakhstan, Turkmenistan and several smaller countries. In theory, all republics were partners in the Union but, in practice, it was ruled from Moscow, the capital of Russia.

Ideological differences between East and West

The Soviet Union, Britain and the USA were ruled according to very different ideologies*. Britain and the USA were capitalist*. The Soviet Union was communist*.

Key terms

Ideology*

A set of shared beliefs. In 1941, the USA and the Soviet Union had different ideologies concerning how a country should be governed and how its society should work.

Capitalism*

Capitalists believe everyone should be free to own property and businesses and make money. The USA's economic ideology was capitalist.

Timeline

East–West relations, 1941–49

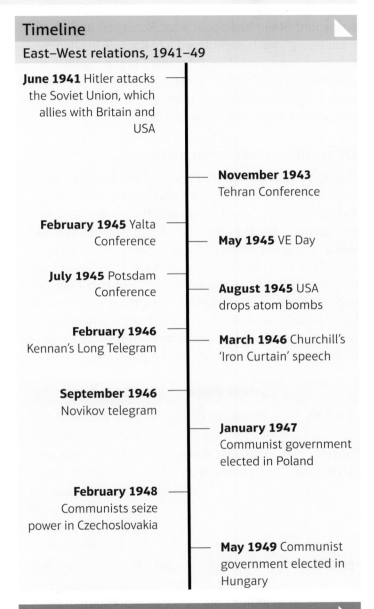

June 1941 Hitler attacks the Soviet Union, which allies with Britain and USA

November 1943 Tehran Conference

February 1945 Yalta Conference

May 1945 VE Day

July 1945 Potsdam Conference

August 1945 USA drops atom bombs

February 1946 Kennan's Long Telegram

March 1946 Churchill's 'Iron Curtain' speech

September 1946 Novikov telegram

January 1947 Communist government elected in Poland

February 1948 Communists seize power in Czechoslovakia

May 1949 Communist government elected in Hungary

Key term

Communism*

Communists believe that all property, including homes and businesses, should belong to the state, to ensure that every member of society has a fair share. Communism is based on the writings of Karl Marx and was the political ideology of the Soviet Union.

Differences between leaders

Roosevelt, Churchill and Stalin (the leaders of the USA, Britain and the Soviet Union in 1941) are often referred to as 'the Big Three', since it was their beliefs and ambitions that dominated world politics from 1941 until Roosevelt's death in 1945. The suspicions that Churchill and Roosevelt had about Stalin (and indeed the suspicions Stalin had about what Roosevelt and Churchill were trying to achieve) played a major role in shaping relations from 1941. The differences in the leaders' personal political beliefs reinforced these suspicions and were a significant factor in the breakdown of relations as the Second World War drew to a close.

Differences between nations

During the 1930s, both the USA and Britain had been very critical of the methods used by Stalin to industrialise the Soviet Union and the terrible cost in human lives that the reforms brought about. But Stalin was a strong opponent of German fascism and so it suited the USA and Britain to work with the Soviet Union to defeat Hitler. Once the war came to an end, however, it was clear that relations between the three countries were likely to become strained. The ideological differences between them meant it was almost impossible to agree on how post-war Europe should be governed.

	Soviet Union	USA & Britain
Politics	Single-party rule	Free elections with a choice of parties
Social structure	Classless society, everyone is equal	Some people have more power than others (because of family background, wealth, education or achievements)
Economy	All property owned by the state, not individuals	Private ownership and a competitive workplace
Rights	Rights of all workers more important than individual rights	Individual freedoms valued but limited by majority opinion

Franklin D. Roosevelt (1882–1945)
President of the USA: 1933–45
He believed strongly in democracy but compromised and formed an alliance with Stalin. After Japan bombed Pearl Harbor in 1941, Roosevelt thought he would need Soviet support against Japan. His desire for Soviet support explains why he was not always as tough in negotiations with Stalin as Churchill would have liked. Roosevelt believed any long-term settlement would only be possible if the Soviet Union was accepted as a superpower and partner in peace.

Winston Churchill (1874–1965)
Prime minister of Britain: 1940–45, 1951–55
As a Conservative from an aristocratic family, Churchill had very traditional values. He believed strongly in the British Empire at a time when many others — including Franklin Roosevelt — thought colonies should be allowed freedom to rule themselves. His political attitudes made him deeply suspicious of Stalin. Throughout the time of The Grand Alliance he saw his role as trying to stop Soviet expansion.

Joseph Stalin (1878–1953)
Leader of the Soviet Union: 1920s–1953
Stalin strengthened one-party rule in the Soviet Union and cut back on people's individual rights. He was convinced that the West wanted to destroy communism, so the Soviet Union had to stand firm in any negotiations with the Western 'superpower', the USA, and its close ally, Britain.

Figure 1.1 Stalin, Churchill and Roosevelt.

Figure 1.2 A summary of US and Soviet attitudes after the Second World War.

A new world order

The Second World War brought about a significant shift in world politics. The 'old powers', like Britain and France, were now less important than they had been. Two new 'superpowers', the Soviet Union and the USA had emerged. Their military and economic strength were responsible for the defeat of Germany but also created a situation that would make future relations very difficult.

The Grand Alliance

The Grand Alliance was formed between the USA, the Soviet Union and Britain to mastermind the defeat of Germany and Japan in the Second World War. The alliance was formed when a force of four million German troops invaded the Soviet Union in June 1941 – despite a non-aggression pact between Germany and the Soviet Union. It is important to remember that, although the three countries had formed an alliance, there was no real change in how they viewed each other. The USA and Britain, in particular, remained suspicious of communism, and Stalin realised that the West would not want to take any actions that made the Soviet Union stronger in the long run.

The leaders of The Grand Alliance nations met three times during the war: at Tehran (1943), Yalta (February 1945) and Potsdam (July 1945).

> **Key terms**
>
> **Democracy***
>
> A political system in which a nation's leaders are chosen in free elections. Both the USA and the Soviet Union said they believed in democracy, but Stalin believed elections had to lead to a communist government, as only The Communist Party represented the working people.
>
> **Satellite state***
>
> A nation that was once independent but is now under the control of another. In the Cold War, 'satellite states' usually describes nations under the political, economic and military control of the Soviet Union.

The significance of the Tehran, Yalta and Potsdam conferences

Tehran, November 1943

The Grand Alliance first met in Tehran to plan a winning strategy to end the war.

Agreements made at Tehran

- The USA and Britain would open a 'second front' by launching an attack on Germany in Western Europe. This would ease pressure on the Eastern Front, where the Soviets were suffering heavy losses. The Germans would then have to withdraw troops from the Soviet Union to fight in the West.
- Stalin would declare war against Japan and supply Soviet troops to help the USA with the war against Japan – but only once the war in Europe was over.

- The Big Three also discussed what would happen to Germany and the countries east of Germany after the war. There was no formal agreement, but it was agreed in principle that the aim of the war was to bring about the unconditional surrender of Germany and that it should remain weak after the war. It was also agreed that Poland should receive land from Germany, but the Soviet Union could keep land it had seized from Poland in 1939. This was very important to Stalin, whose ultimate aim was to secure his western border after the war.

- There was a general agreement that an international body should be set up to settle disputes through discussion and negotiation, rather than war. This laid the ground for the future formation of the United Nations.

The Tehran conference had an important impact on international relations. Stalin had arrived in Tehran concerned that the USA and Britain were deliberately delaying a 'second front' against Germany so that the Soviet Union could be further weakened by having to fight a fierce defensive war in the East. So he was pleased with the agreement to open a 'second front' in the West. Churchill was less pleased because he had wanted to open the 'second front' in the Balkans, not in the West. However, Roosevelt sided with Stalin on this.

So there was some tension between the USA and Britain – especially as Roosevelt seemed at times to view British colonialism* as more of a threat to world peace than the Soviet Union. It seemed that good relations between Roosevelt and Stalin might create a position where the Big Three was becoming the Big Two and, after 1945, the USA and the Soviet Union would be the only global superpowers.

Yalta, February 1945

Two years after the Tehran Conference, the Big Three held a second meeting to discuss winning the war and the government of post-war Europe at Yalta in the Soviet Union. By then, the 'second front' had been launched in France and British and American-led forces were pushing the Germans back towards Berlin. More importantly, the Soviets had defeated the Germans in the Soviet Union and now had control of most of Central and Eastern Europe. Stalin was determined to keep the territory he had won between the Soviet border and Germany as a cushion against future German invasions.

Agreements made at Yalta

- After the war, Germany would be split into four zones. They would each be controlled by a different power, the USA, Britain, France and the Soviet Union. Germany would pay $20 billion in reparations*, half of which would go to the Soviet Union. The Nazi Party would be banned and war criminals prosecuted.

- A United Nations would be set up, with its first meeting on 25 April 1945. All nations could join, but the USA and France did not agree with Stalin's suggestion that all 16 Soviet republics should be given individual membership. Instead, Russia, the Ukraine and Belarus were admitted.

> ### Key terms
>
> **Colonialism***
>
> Economic, political and cultural control of another country.
>
> **Reparations***
>
> Payments in money or goods, after a war, from the losing country to the victors. Reparations are compensation for loss of life and damage to land and the economy.

Source A

A photograph showing the Big Three – Winston Churchill, Franklin Roosevelt and Josef Stalin – at the Yalta conference in February 1945.

- Stalin agreed to join in the war against Japan, three months after the defeat of Germany.
- Stalin agreed that future governments of countries in Eastern Europe would be decided in free elections.
- Poland proved to be the stumbling block at the conference. It was agreed that the borders of Poland would be returned to their position in 1921 (which would give the Soviet Union significant gains) and that there would be free elections. However, Stalin expected those elections to bring about a pro-communist government, whereas the British supported the non-communist London Poles*.

Roosevelt and Stalin were pleased to get agreement on free elections and the United Nations, but the issue of Poland was to prove a difficult one to solve in future discussions.

Potsdam, July–August 1945

Although the conference at Potsdam, near Berlin, took place only a few months after Yalta, a number of crucial events during that time influenced the mood of the conference.

There was a change of personnel

- Roosevelt died in April 1945 and was replaced by Harry S. Truman.
- Winston Churchill and the Conservative Party lost the 1945 general election.
- The new Labour prime minister was Clement Attlee.

Other world events

- Germany had surrendered in May 1945.
- Scientists in the USA had developed an atomic bomb (which they tested successfully the day after the conference began).

Key terms

London Poles*

A group of politicians who left Poland after the German invasion in 1939 and formed a government-in-exile, first in Paris and then in London.

Veto*

Forbid or refuse. Permanent members of the UN Security Council can stop resolutions being passed with a single 'no' vote, even if all the other members think it should be passed.

- The United Nations had been created in the Treaty of San Francisco in June 1945. Eventually, 51 members signed the treaty. The USA, the Soviet Union, France, Britain and China were made permanent members of the United Nations Security Council, with the power to veto* resolutions.

The new personalities involved meant that relations between the three leaders at Potsdam were very different from the earlier conferences.

Compared to Roosevelt and Churchill, Truman and Attlee were new to diplomatic discussions. It was much harder for them to get their way with Stalin.

Truman was determined to take a 'get tough' approach with Stalin and deliberately delayed the date of the conference until the atomic bomb was ready (see page 14). He thought this would give him an edge on discussions.

As a newly-elected prime minister, Attlee's main concern was to return to Britain to take charge and he did not want the talks to drag on.

Although the development of the atom bomb soured relations and the defeat of Germany had taken away the need to work against a common enemy, the allies did find some common ground.

Agreements made at Potsdam

- Germany would be divided into four zones, administered by the Soviet Union, the USA, Britain and France, but the German economy would be run as a whole.
- Berlin would also be divided into four zones, controlled by different countries, even though it was based well inside Soviet-controlled Germany.

The Soviet Union wanted Germany to pay heavy reparations, but Truman was concerned that this would make it harder for the German economy to recover. It was agreed that each administering country should take reparations from its own zone. As the Soviet Union controlled the poorest zone, it was allowed to take a quarter of the industrial equipment from the other zones.

Agreement was not reached over the government of Eastern Europe. Truman objected to the control that the Soviet Union had over the countries it had liberated from Nazi rule. He was beginning to see the Red Army as an army of occupation. However, without risking further war, there was little Truman could do.

Truman also objected to the arrangements for Poland and the borders that had previously been agreed. He wanted to see a new government with less communist influence.

Figure 1.3 The post-war division of Germany into four parts: the Soviet, French, British and American sectors.

Exam tip

This question asks about 'consequences', so you will need to think about what difference the decisions made to relations at that time. Don't just give details of what happened, explain why the decision was important. It was agreed that Germany should be divided into four zones. How did that **affect** international relations? (See pages 97–98 for examples of an average and high-scoring answer to the question.)

Activities

1. Create a table to summarise the Tehran, Yalta and Potsdam conferences. Label the columns: Tehran, Yalta and Potsdam. Label the rows: 'Date', 'Leaders present', 'Key decisions', 'Impact of decisions on relations between the Big Three'. Fill out the table in as much detail as you can.
2. Discuss in small groups which impact from your table had the most effect on relations between the Big Three.
3. Write a paragraph explaining why you made this choice.

Exam-style question, Section A

Explain **two** consequences of the decisions made by The Grand Alliance at the Yalta Conference in February 1945. **8 marks**

US–Soviet relations 1945–46: the wartime alliance unravels

Although the members of The Grand Alliance agreed on many issues at the Tehran, Yalta and Potsdam conferences, by the end of Postdam, it was clear that there were now significant issues that they could not agree on. In particular, Stalin wanted control of Eastern Europe to ensure the security of the Soviet Union. In his view, getting control of Eastern Europe was a reasonable defensive measure. But Truman believed that Stalin was trying to spread communism and looked upon Stalin's ambitions as examples of communist aggression. In the years 1945–46, this basic disagreement and mutual suspicion turned the wartime alliance into peacetime hostility.

The impact of the atom bomb on US–Soviet relations

On 6 August 1945, the USA exploded an atom bomb over the Japanese city of Hiroshima. A second was released over Nagasaki on 9 August. The blast at Hiroshima was equivalent to over 12,000 tons of the TNT (explosive material) used in ordinary bombs. It is estimated that over 120,000 Japanese civilians were killed by the two bombs.

Some historians argue that the USA could have won the war against Japan without using nuclear weapons. They say the USA really used the bombs to establish a stronger bargaining position with the Soviet Union. This is only an opinion, but it is certainly true that knowing the USA could make atomic bombs made Truman feel more confident and determined in the negotiations at Potsdam. Also, the development of the atomic bomb made the countries of Western Europe feel more secure about placing themselves under American protection, rather than looking to reach agreement with the Soviet Union.

But, if the Americans hoped that having the atomic bomb would make it easier to persuade Stalin to allow Eastern European countries more freedom, they were wrong. Actually, Stalin now felt even more determined to make the Soviet Union secure. His immediate aim was to create a buffer zone of countries sympathetic to communism between Germany and the Soviet Union's western borders. So, overall, the effect the development of the atomic bomb had on US–Soviet relations was completely opposite to what the Americans had hoped for.

The USA's nuclear monopoly did not last. Soviet scientists were already working on their own version of the atom bomb and their first successful test was on 29 August 1949, just four years after the USA. By 1964, Britain, France and China also had the atomic bomb.

The bomb dramatically increased Cold War tensions. A war that used atomic weapons could kill millions of people and destroy the world many times over. But, equally, the terrible consequences of using an atomic bomb may have made both the USA and the Soviet Union more reluctant to go to war. Instead they entered an arms race, in which each side tried to make sure their nuclear weapons were more powerful than those of their rival.

Activities ?

1 Look at Source B in a small group and discuss why the cartoon is called 'The Big Fourth'. What is 'The Big Fourth'? What does the shadow represent?

2 The cartoon was published in July 1945. If Zec had drawn it on 10 August, how might it have been different? Describe the alternative cartoon in words or draw your own version.

Source B

This cartoon, 'The Big Fourth', by the British cartoonist Philip Zec, was published in the *Daily Mirror* on 17 July 1945.

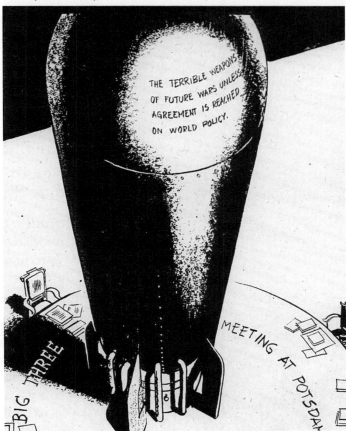

Rising tensions: the Kennan Long telegram and the Novikov telegram

Both Truman and Stalin feared that the break-up of The Grand Alliance might lead to future conflict. They wanted to know what their rivals were thinking and, in 1946, both asked their embassies to report on attitudes in each other's countries. These reports came in the form of telegrams – a written message sent over a telegraph line.

Source C

From the 'Long Telegram' sent from Moscow to Washington by the US ambassador to the Soviet Union, George Kennan, on 22 February 1946.

We have here a political force committed fanatically to the belief that... it is desirable and necessary that... our traditional way of life be destroyed, the international authority of our state be broken, if Soviet power is to be secure... But... the problem is within our power to solve... without... military conflict.

Soviet attitudes: George Kennan's Long Telegram

George Kennan, America's ambassador in Moscow, had lived and worked in the Soviet Union as a diplomat. When he sent a telegram discussing US–Soviet relations, his views were taken seriously by the American government. While most telegrams were very short, Kennan's telegram was more like a letter, so his message became known as the Long Telegram.

It contained a message that worried the American government. He reported that Stalin wanted to see the destruction of capitalism and that he felt the world outside the Soviet Union was hostile and looking to destroy communism. However, Kennan also believed that the Soviet Union was not suicidal, so if faced with strong resistance, would back down. This was a really important message, which played a key role in American policy towards the Soviet Union in the coming years. The American government believed there should be a determined policy of 'containment' to stop communism spreading.

US attitudes: the Novikov Telegram

Nikolai Novikov was a Soviet diplomat working in Washington. His telegram to the government in Moscow (discovered recently in a Soviet archive) shows that the Soviets thought equally poorly of the West: each side distrusted the other.

Novikov's telegram said the USA wanted to use their massive military power to dominate the world. He believed that, since Roosevelt's death, the Americans no longer wanted to co-operate with the Soviet Union and the American people would support their government if this led to war. Such a view had a major impact in Moscow. If this was how the USA was thinking, it was vital to develop as much protection as possible in Eastern Europe.

Source E

From a speech given by Winston Churchill on 5 March 1946 at Westminster College, Fulton, Missouri. Here he describes the Soviet Union's growing control over Eastern Europe.

From Stettin in the Baltic to Trieste in the Adriatic, an iron curtain has descended across the Continent. Behind that line lie all the capitals of the ancient states of Central and Eastern Europe... all are subject in one form or another, not only to Soviet influence but to a very high and, in some cases, increasing measure of control from Moscow.

Source D

From the 'Novikov Telegram' sent from Washington to Moscow by Nikolai Novikov, Soviet Ambassador to the USA, on 27 September 1946.

US foreign policy has been characterized in the postwar period by a desire for world domination. All these steps to preserve the great military potential are not an end in itself, of course. They are intended only to prepare conditions to win world domination in a new war being planned by the most warlike circles of American imperialism... .

A British point-of-view: Winston Churchill's 'Iron Curtain' speech

In March 1946, Winston Churchill was no longer prime minister but he still had enormous influence. On a visit to Fulton, Missouri he gave a speech that is now seen as a defining moment in US–Soviet relations. In the speech he made it plain that he thought the Soviet Union was a threat to freedom and world peace. He was provoked to make this speech by the fact that communist governments had recently been set up in Hungary, Poland, Romania and Bulgaria.

Churchill was speaking in the USA and must have cleared his speech with Truman first. So Stalin interpreted what Churchill said as reflecting American beliefs too. The speech, along with the Novikov telegram, increased tension and mistrust, and led the Soviet Union to strengthen its forces and step up a campaign of anti-Western propaganda. Whether he intended it or not, Churchill's speech intensified the growing hostility between East and West.

The creation of Soviet satellite states in Eastern Europe

In 1944 and 1945, the Soviet Red Army freed many countries in Eastern Europe from the Nazis as it advanced west towards Germany. When the war was over, Stalin was reluctant to give up control of these countries as they were a useful buffer zone between the Soviet Union and Germany. He turned them into satellite states with communist governments and little genuine independence from the Soviet Union. Truman saw this as evidence that the Soviet Union wanted to spread communism worldwide, and relations between the USA and the Soviet Union became worse.

Activities ?

1 What term does Churchill use in his speech to describe the imaginary line between East and West in Europe?

2 With a partner re-read Sources C, D and E. Try to summarise the message in each source into just one or two sentences.

3 Set up a debate, with one group representing the USA and the other representing the Soviet Union. Argue that the worsening of relations after 1941 was not your fault, but was all down to 'the other side'. What will you say?

Source F

A photograph of Klement Gottwald speaking at a communist rally in Prague, February 1948. After a coalition government collapsed, Gottwald became president of a communist Czechoslovakia.

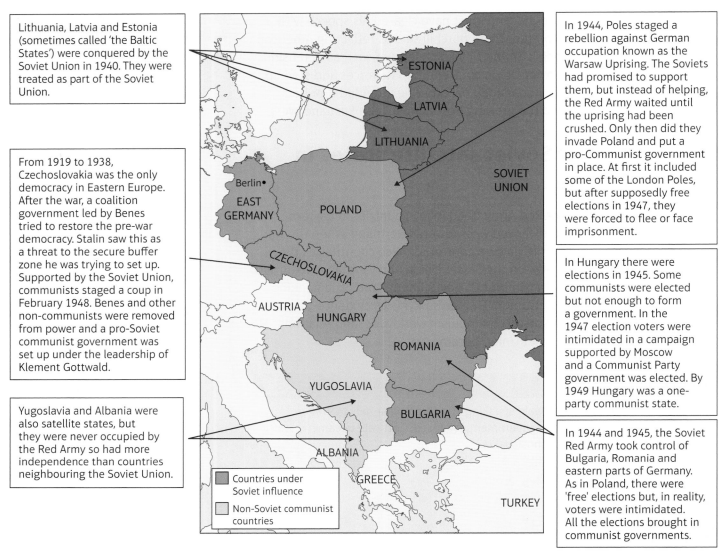

Lithuania, Latvia and Estonia (sometimes called 'the Baltic States') were conquered by the Soviet Union in 1940. They were treated as part of the Soviet Union.

From 1919 to 1938, Czechoslovakia was the only democracy in Eastern Europe. After the war, a coalition government led by Benes tried to restore the pre-war democracy. Stalin saw this as a threat to the secure buffer zone he was trying to set up. Supported by the Soviet Union, communists staged a coup in February 1948. Benes and other non-communists were removed from power and a pro-Soviet communist government was set up under the leadership of Klement Gottwald.

Yugoslavia and Albania were also satellite states, but they were never occupied by the Red Army so had more independence than countries neighbouring the Soviet Union.

In 1944, Poles staged a rebellion against German occupation known as the Warsaw Uprising. The Soviets had promised to support them, but instead of helping, the Red Army waited until the uprising had been crushed. Only then did they invade Poland and put a pro-Communist government in place. At first it included some of the London Poles, but after supposedly free elections in 1947, they were forced to flee or face imprisonment.

In Hungary there were elections in 1945. Some communists were elected but not enough to form a government. In the 1947 election voters were intimidated in a campaign supported by Moscow and a Communist Party government was elected. By 1949 Hungary was a one-party communist state.

In 1944 and 1945, the Soviet Red Army took control of Bulgaria, Romania and eastern parts of Germany. As in Poland, there were 'free' elections but, in reality, voters were intimidated. All the elections brought in communist governments.

Countries under Soviet influence

Non-Soviet communist countries

Figure 1.4 How the countries of Eastern Europe became Soviet satellite states.

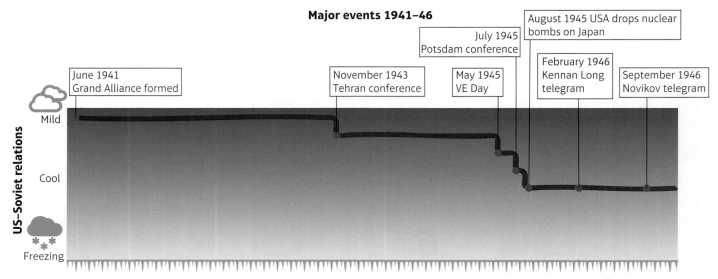

Major events 1941–46

June 1941
Grand Alliance formed

November 1943
Tehran conference

May 1945
VE Day

July 1945
Potsdam conference

August 1945 USA drops nuclear bombs on Japan

February 1946
Kennan Long telegram

September 1946
Novikov telegram

US–Soviet relations

Mild

Cool

Freezing

Figure 1.5 Declining relations between the USA and the Soviet Union, 1941–46.

Exam-style question, Section A

Write a narrative account analysing the key events of the Soviet takeover of the satellite states in the period 1944–48.

You may use the following in your answer:

- the Warsaw Uprising
- the communist takeover of Czechoslovakia.

You **must** also use information of your own. **8 marks**

Exam tip

To score well on this type of question, your account needs to link events together and explain how one leads to another in a logical and structured way.

Summary

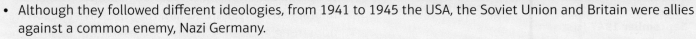

- Although they followed different ideologies, from 1941 to 1945 the USA, the Soviet Union and Britain were allies against a common enemy, Nazi Germany.
- In 1943, the Big Three began talks (at Tehran) about how to end the war and how to deal with Germany after the war. Final agreement on the division of Germany into four zones of occupation came at Yalta in 1945.
- Victory in Europe (VE) Day saw Allied victory over the Nazis and left the Soviet Red Army in control of what became the satellite states: Poland, Czechoslovakia, Bulgaria, Romania, Hungary, Yugoslavia and the Soviet zone of Germany.
- In August 1945, the USA exploded two atomic bombs over Japan and a new age in international relations, dominated by these powerful new weapons, began.
- By 1946, the USA and the Soviet Union had lost trust in each other. Both were convinced that their countries' ideologies were under threat because of the aggressive foreign policies of their rivals.

Checkpoint

Strengthen

S1 How is 'cold' war different from conventional war?

S2 Which heads of state attended the Tehran and Potsdam conferences?

S3 What did the Allies plan for Germany at Yalta? Is this what finally happened?

S4 In your own words, explain the differences between communism and capitalism.

Challenge

C1 Describe how relations between the USA, Britain and the Soviet Union changed between Tehran and Potsdam.

C2 How did the development and use of the atomic bomb affect East–West relations?

C3 What do the Long (Kennan) and Novikov telegrams show about mutual distrust between the Soviet Union and the West?

How confident do you feel about your answers to these questions? Form a small group and discuss any questions you are not sure about. Look for the answers in this section. Now rewrite your answers as a group.

1.2 The development of the Cold War

Timeline
Growing East–West divisions, 1947–49

March 1947 Truman Doctrine announced

June 1947 Marshall Aid plan announced

September 1947 First Cominform meeting

February 1948 Communist takeover of Czechoslovakia

June 1948 Berlin blockade is set up

January 1949 Comecon established

April 1949 NATO formed

September 1949 Official founding of the Federal Republic of Germany

October 1949 German Democratic Republic established

May 1955 Warsaw Pact formed

The impact of the Truman Doctrine and Marshall Plan

Kennan's Long Telegram (see page 15) had confirmed Truman's worst fears. It said the Soviet Union intended to spread communism throughout Europe. Truman's military advisers assured him that the Soviet Union was not strong enough to fight a successful war against the West, but Truman knew that the Soviet Union might not need to go to war to increase its territory and power. After the Second World War, many European countries were in ruins. Homes, factories and infrastructure like roads and railways had been destroyed. In these economic conditions, communism looked very attractive to poorer members of society because, in a communist state, the wealth of the richest people would be redistributed and shared by all. So Stalin did not need to fight a war. He just needed to influence the discontented people of Europe to support communism and help set up communist governments.

The Truman Doctrine – stating the US position

The USA had hoped that wealthier European countries, such as Britain, might be able to help rebuild Europe's shattered economies (and make communism look like a less attractive option). But, after six years of war, Britain was nearly bankrupt and aid to other countries was becoming impossible. When the British government announced in 1947 that it could no longer provide military support to the Greek government against communist guerrillas, President Truman decided it was time to take action.

On 12 March 1947, President Truman delivered a speech to the US Congress (see Source A on page 21). The speech was officially given to announce an economic aid package to Greece and Turkey. Truman announced that the US would provide $400 million in aid to Greece and Turkey and sent American civilian and military personnel to the region.

Extend your knowledge

The Greek Civil War

During the Second World War, the German occupation of Greece was resisted by two separate groups in Greece, a communist group and a pro-royalist group. After the Germans left, the two groups fell out. The British restored the Greek monarchy and put down a communist rebellion. When the communists renewed their fight in 1946, the British tried to suppress them, but asked the USA to take over in 1947. The communists were finally defeated in 1949 and fled to Albania.

However, Truman also used the opportunity to make a clear statement of what he saw as the differences between democracy and communism. He spoke of two alternative ways of life between which every nation must choose. The first way, he said, offered majority rule and freedom from political oppression. The second was for the will of the minority to be forced upon the majority, which Truman said was what communism did. Truman believed choosing democracy over communism was like choosing good over evil. He said communism should not be allowed to grow and that the USA was prepared to send troops and economic aid to those countries trying to resist it.

These ideas became known as 'the Truman Doctrine' and signalled the beginnings of a new approach to international relations for the USA. Before the Second World War, the USA had followed a policy of isolationism*. This policy was now abandoned. The USA was setting itself up as the leader of the fight against communism and isolationism was replaced with containment*.

Source A

From the Truman Doctrine speech delivered on 12 March 1947 to the US Congress. Immediately before this extract, Truman described American-style democracy as majority rule and freedom from political oppression.

The second way of life is based upon the will of a minority forcibly imposed upon the majority. It relies upon terror and oppression, a controlled press and radio; fixed elections, and the suppression of personal freedoms. I believe that our help should be primarily through economic and financial aid which is essential to economic stability and orderly political processes.

Key terms

Isolationism*

Staying apart, not getting involved in the affairs of others. The USA followed a policy of isolationism after the First World War. It was forced to abandon this policy in 1941 when Japan bombed Pearl Harbour. However, in 1945, when the war ended, many Americans hoped the country would return to isolationism.

Containment*

Limiting the spread of something. In US foreign policy (during the Cold War), 'containment' meant preventing the spread of communism outside a small number of countries.

The Marshall Plan – fighting communism with financial aid

Source B

A photograph of American and British officials watching Caribbean sugar, sent under the Marshall Plan, being unloaded at Woolwich Docks.

The USA had not suffered damage to its infrastructure and industry during the war in the same way as European countries had, so it was well placed to provide economic aid to Europe. Three months after Truman's speech, details were set out on how that aid would be provided in a speech by the US secretary of state, George Marshall.

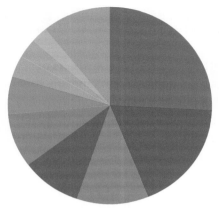

Key

- ■ United Kingdom $3,297 million
- ■ France $2,296 million
- ■ West Germany $1,448 million
- ■ Italy $1,204 million
- ■ Netherlands $1,128 million
- ■ Belgium & Luxembourg $777 million
- ■ Austria $468 million
- ■ Denmark $385 million
- ■ Greece $376 million
- ■ Other nations $1,352 million

Figure 1.6 The money given to European nations under the Marshall Plan was shared out according to population and how industrialised they were before the war.

The Marshall Plan was a practical outcome of the Truman Doctrine: providing economic aid to help war-torn countries in order to stop communism from taking over in Western Europe. Between 1948 and 1952, the USA gave $12.7 billion dollars of aid, in addition to $13 billion already given by the USA before the Marshall Plan went into action.

The economic impact of Marshall Aid in Western Europe was enormous, although it took until the 1950s for the full effects to be seen. The British foreign secretary, Ernest Bevin, called it 'a lifeline to sinking men, giving hope where there was none'.

In the USA, there was much debate about whether to offer aid to the Soviet Union and the satellite states. It was decided that it could be offered but (as in Western Europe) countries would first have to agree to a thorough review of their finances. However, the USA knew Stalin would not allow this so, in practice, Eastern European countries did not benefit from the Marshall Plan.

Source C

From a speech made by US Secretary of State, George Marshall, on 5 June 1947. Marshall said Europe could not possibly meet its own needs for food and essential products for the next three–four years and needed substantial help.

Our policy is directed not against any country or doctrine but against hunger, poverty, desperation and chaos. Its purpose should be the revival of a working economy in the world so as to permit the emergence of political and social conditions in which free institutions can exist... .

Extend your knowledge

Smaller-scale Marshall Aid

Marshall Aid was not just loans and grants to governments. It also involved making direct grants to groups in need. So it included nets for Norwegian fishermen, mules for Greek farmers and food for starving people. One hungry boy who received free soup from the back of a lorry in his schoolyard was called Helmut Kohl. He grew up to be the first Chancellor of a reunited Germany after the Cold War.

'Dollar imperialism' – the Soviet response

President Truman saw his new policy as a defensive measure to contain communism. Not surprisingly, Stalin did not see it like that at all. He believed the Truman Doctrine showed that the USA was trying to extend its influence in Europe. He also thought it was undermining the international role of the United Nations by suggesting that it was America's job to protect the world. Stalin argued that the Marshall Plan was a way of using economic might to divide Europe in two and establish an American economic empire in Europe. The Soviets called this 'dollar imperialism'.

The Truman Doctrine and the Marshall Plan had a huge impact on international relations from 1947.

- Any lingering belief that there was still a Grand Alliance was gone, as the USA had now set itself up in direct opposition to the communist Soviet Union – and invited other nations to join it.
- Stalin's suspicions of the West were reinforced. He believed he now had evidence that the USA was trying to crush the Soviet Union.
- The Marshall Plan successfully tied Western European countries into supporting the USA. As Stalin rejected it (and set up his own economic plan, Comecon – see below), Europe was now divided into two economic and political camps.
- The history of Europe for the next 50 years became one of intense rivalry and attempts to win diplomatic and political victories over political opponents.

Source D

From a speech by the Soviet foreign minister, Andrey Vyshinsky, given at the United Nations in September 1947.

It is becoming more and more evident that the implementation of the Marshall Plan will mean placing European countries under the economic and political control of the United States and direct interference in those countries. Moreover, this plan is an attempt to split Europe into two camps, and with the help of Britain and France, to complete the formation of a group of countries hostile to the interests of the democratic countries.

The formation of Cominform and Comecon

The Marshall Plan set Stalin an economic and political challenge. He therefore created two new organisations for the communist countries of Europe, Cominform and Comecon:

Cominform, 1947

Cominform (the Communist Information Bureau) was a political organisation set up on Stalin's orders on 22 September 1947. It had nine members: the Communist Party of the Soviet Union, and the Communist Parties of the satellite states of Bulgaria, Czechoslovakia, Hungary, Poland and Romania along with Yugoslavia, France and Italy. The strongest support for Cominform came from the Yugoslav communists under the leadership of Tito, so its headquarters were established in Belgrade. However, growing tension between Yugoslavia and the Soviet Union led to the expulsion of Yugoslavia from Cominform in June 1948. The headquarters were then moved to Bucharest in Romania.

The new body gave Stalin a way of directing and controlling the governments of the satellite states. He wanted to ensure that they not only followed communism, but also took orders from Moscow. The satellite states were encouraged to concentrate on trading with other Cominform members and all contact with non-communist countries was discouraged. At Cominform's first meeting it rejected the Marshall Plan and began to spread propaganda accusing America of being no different from Nazi Germany.

Comecon, 1949

Stalin wanted communist states to keep their independence from capitalist governments and did not want the US to become influential in Eastern Europe, so he would not allow the satellite states to accept Marshall Aid. He also knew that he needed to offer a positive alternative if he was to keep the satellite nations under his control.

He therefore created Comecon (the Council for Mutual Economic Assistance) to provide aid in line with communist principles. Comecon was established on 25 January 1949, two years after the Marshall Plan was announced. Its members were the Soviet Union, Bulgaria, Czechoslovakia, Hungary, Poland, Romania and East Germany. Albania joined the following year.

Comecon was in direct competition with the Marshall Plan and aimed to support economic development in its member states. At first Comecon's main activities were arranging trade and credit agreements between member countries. After 1953 the Soviet Union used Comecon to try to organise industrial planning across all the satellite states. Each state had a Five Year Plan, nationalised industry and collectivised agriculture. Trade with the USA and Western Europe was discouraged in favour of trade with the Soviet Union and other member states. So, for example, Bulgaria's trade with other Comecon members increased from around 10% in the 1930s to over 90% in 1951.

Stalin formed Cominform and Comecon in response to the threat he believed the Marshall Plan posed to the Soviet Union. However, his actions actually increased tension and played a significant part in the USA and Western European countries creating a new military alliance, the North Atlantic Treaty Organisation (NATO), in April 1949.

The 1948 Berlin Crisis – testing the West

Europe was now divided into two distinct political and economic camps. Soon there would also be two military camps, but first Stalin wanted to see just how determined the West really was.

Germany divided

At Potsdam, The Grand Alliance agreed to divide Germany, and its capital Berlin, into four separate occupation zones administered by the Soviet Union, the USA, Britain and France. The division was meant to be temporary but ended up lasting for many years. The Allied Control Commission (ACC) was the central organisation for the four zones. There were soldiers on the streets and, in Berlin, military checkpoints between zones.

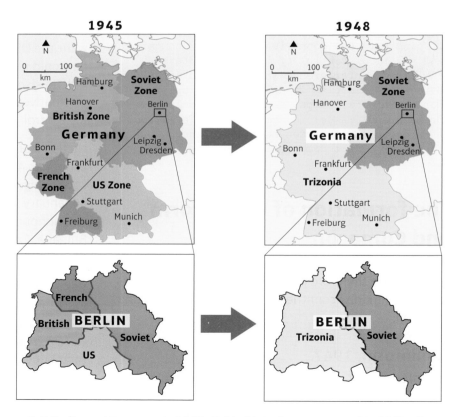

Figure 1.7 Berlin and Germany in 1945, divided into four zones, and in 1948, after the Western zones were joined together as Trizonia.

There were disagreements between the occupying powers. The three Western countries and the Soviet Union had different ways of looking at Germany. The Soviets wanted to take as much material as possible back to help rebuild the Soviet Union, whilst the Western countries wanted to build up Germany's economy. In March 1948, talks between the foreign ministers of the occupying powers broke down and the Soviets stormed out.

Uniting the Western zones

With the Soviets no longer co-operating, the remaining allies (the USA, Britain and France) had to decide how to run their part of Germany. The British and Americans had already combined their zones into 'Bizonia' in 1947 and, in March 1948, the French added theirs to create 'Trizonia'. Although this was never their intention, the result was that Germany and Berlin were now split into two parts, western Trizonia and eastern Soviet-controlled Germany.

Then, in June 1948, the three Allies created a single currency, the Deutschmark, to give Trizonia economic unity. The decision to introduce the Deutschmark took place at an ACC meeting in Berlin. The Soviets were furious about the decision for two reasons:

- The new single currency in Trizonia created a separate economic unit from the East.
- It acknowledged that there were in effect two Germanys: West and East.

To Stalin, this was a further example of the West 'ganging up' on the Soviet Union. He saw the formation of Trizonia as a means of developing the three zones more effectively and deliberately forcing the Soviet zone into poverty. He was now even more determined to stand firm and protect Soviet interests in Germany. He believed Germany should be one united country and that it should follow communist ideology.

The Berlin blockade

Stalin knew that the Western-occupied zones of Berlin were vulnerable, as they were entirely surrounded by Soviet-occupied territory. In addition, there were just two agreed land routes and two air routes or 'corridors' across the Soviet zone of Germany to Western-occupied Berlin.

In June 1948, Stalin decided to shut off the land routes across Soviet-controlled Germany into Berlin, in what has

Extend your knowledge

German attitudes to the Soviets

Stalin hoped that, after the war, a united Germany might become communist. But this was very unlikely. Even in the Soviet zone, the Soviets were not popular. As the Red Army advanced into Germany at the end of the Second World War, its soldiers carried out brutal atrocities in revenge for what the Nazis had done in the Soviet Union. This created deep resentment amongst many Germans.

become known as the 'Berlin blockade'. He wanted to show the USA, Britain and France that a divided Germany would not work. The main section of Trizonia in western Germany would no longer be able to communicate with the capital Berlin and the people of Berlin would soon run short of food. If the blockade was successful, Stalin would win a huge propaganda success at the expense of the West. It might also mean that the Western powers would give up control of their zones in Berlin and allow the whole of the capital to be controlled by the Soviet Union. This was a direct challenge to Truman – Stalin knew he could not ignore the blockade because of his recent speech about defending the world from communism (see page 21).

The West knew that an attempt to force supplies to Berlin along the closed land routes would be seen as a potential act of war and might lead to direct military confrontation. However, if they flew supplies into their zones in Berlin, the only way they could be stopped was if Stalin had the planes shot down. That would make him the aggressor and Truman doubted that Stalin was prepared to go that far.

Operation Vittles: the Berlin Airlift

The Western Allies launched Operation Vittles, better known as the Berlin Airlift. They flew food, coal and other necessities, assembled in the Allied zones, along the air corridors. The pilots took a huge risk as they could not be sure the Soviets would not shoot them down.

The people of West Berlin and Western troops in the city joined forces to build a new runway at the old airport Berlin-Tempelhof, and a whole new airport at Berlin-Tegel, so that supplies could be landed in the Western zones. Ordinary citizens helped to unload the planes and hand out the essential supplies to all who needed them. The Americans were soon able to fly in at least 1,000 tonnes of

Extend your knowledge

Operation Little Vittles
Whilst landing supplies at Tempelhof airport, the American pilot Gail Halvorsen saw children watching from the fence. He decided that on his next flight he would parachute-drop sweets to them. Soon other pilots did the same. Their actions were nicknamed 'Operation Little Vittles'.

Activities ?

1 List the practical steps the British and US armed forces took to set up the Berlin airlift. What did citizens of Berlin do to help the airlift succeed?

2 Write a short paragraph explaining why the USA was so determined to keep the Western zones of Berlin out of Soviet hands.

3 In a small group, discuss what the results might have been if:

   a The Western Allies had not launched the Berlin Airlift.

   b Stalin had shot down the first planes flying supplies to Berlin.

supplies every day and the British achieved a similar rate. In the peak month of flying, January 1949, no fewer than 170,000 tonnes of supplies were sent into Berlin by Western aircraft.

On 9 May 1949, nearly a year later, the Soviets gave in and lifted the blockade. The airlift had worked. Amazingly, there were no Allied casualties, military or civilian. West Berlin had survived. Stalin's attempt to win a propaganda victory over Britain, France and the USA had backfired. The West had responded in a peaceful way to what now looked like an unwise and aggressive act by Stalin.

Source E

A photograph of children watching as a supply plane arrives in Berlin during the Berlin Airlift.

The formation of East and West Germany

After the Berlin blockade, it was clear that the division of Germany would continue. The Western allies quickly moved to create a separate West Germany.

Federal Republic of Germany (West Germany)

- 23 May 1949: Just three days after the end of the blockade, the USA, Britain and France permitted their zones to come together as a state known as the Federal Republic of Germany.
- 14 August 1949: Germans in the new country were allowed to elect their own parliament, called the *Bundestag*.
- 15 September 1949: the first democratically elected chancellor of the Federal Republic, Konrad Adenauer took office.
- The Federal Republic's new capital was Bonn. The new country was much bigger than East Germany.
- The three Western-controlled zones of Berlin continued and became known as West Berlin.

German Democratic Republic (East Germany)

Stalin responded by creating the German Democratic Republic in October 1949. Only the communist bloc countries recognised it as a nation. The Federal Republic refused to recognise that Germany had been split in two until the 1970s.

For the next 40 years, people would talk about West Germany and East Germany but, for most of this time, each German regarded their own state as the only real one.

The creation of two armed camps

NATO, 1949

Stalin's threat to Berlin and the communist takeover in Czechoslovakia, which happened in the same year, persuaded the Western powers that they needed a formal military alliance to protect themselves from the Soviet Union. They also wanted to send Stalin a message about their determination to stand firm against communism.

In April 1949, the USA, Britain, France and nine other Western countries joined together in the North Atlantic Treaty Organisation (NATO). The members of NATO agreed that, if any member was attacked, all members of NATO would come to its assistance. The British foreign secretary, Ernest Bevin had played a major part in bringing about this alliance. He made a speech in the British parliament in which he said that European countries would welcome American involvement and called on other Western European countries to reach out to the USA.

It was not inevitable that the USA would get involved directly in the defence of Western Europe after the Second World War. The Truman Doctrine said the USA would offer assistance, but the creation of a formal military alliance was a major step beyond this. NATO resulted in an ongoing American military presence in Europe throughout the Cold War, which has continued right up to the present day.

The Warsaw Pact, 1955

When the German Federal Republic (West Germany) was allowed to join NATO in May 1955, the Soviet Union's fears were increased. Now there was a real danger of an armed and powerful Germany on the borders of Soviet-controlled Eastern Europe. Within a week of West Germany joining NATO, the Soviet Union formed an equivalent communist defensive military alliance – the Warsaw Pact. The members were the Soviet Union, Poland, Czechoslovakia, Hungary, Romania, Bulgaria, Albania and the German Democratic Republic (East Germany). These countries became known as the 'Eastern bloc'. Although the Warsaw Pact had many member states, the leadership was entirely Soviet and the alliance was under the command of the Soviet Union.

Source F

An extract from the NATO Charter. Article 5 stated:

The Parties agree that an armed attack against one or more of them in Europe or North America shall be considered an attack against them all and consequently they agree that, if such an armed attack occurs, each of them... will assist the Party or Parties so attacked by taking such action as it deems necessary, including the use of armed force, to restore and maintain the security of the North Atlantic area.

There was now no doubt that Europe was, in reality, two Europes. One was under the protection of the USA and working to defeat communism. The other was led by the Soviet Union and seeking to extend communist control. The confrontation and hostility between these two camps would drive international relations for the next 35 years.

Exam-style question, Section A

Explain **two** of the following:

- the importance of the Truman Doctrine for the development of the Cold War in the years 1947–55
- the importance of the Berlin Blockade for the future of Germany
- the importance of the formation of NATO for relations between the USA and the Soviet Union.   **16 marks**

Exam tip

Remember that this question is not asking for a description of an event or policy. It is asking why that event or policy was important. What difference did it make? Also, remember to focus on the second part of each bullet point. So, for the second bullet point, focus on the 'future of Germany'. Don't waste time discussing, for example, how the Berlin Blockade affected relations between the USA and the Soviet Union.

Activity ?

Challenge a partner to see who can give the best one-minute speech about 'How the Cold War developed, 1947–55'. As you listen to your partner's speech, list any important events you think have been missed. What would you include in a short summary?

Summary

- In the Truman Doctrine, Truman promised to defend democratic countries against communism.
- George Marshall, the US secretary of state, promised massive aid to Europe, launching the Marshall Plan.
- Western European countries welcomed the Marshall Plan, but Soviet-controlled countries were not allowed to accept aid. The Soviet Union set up Cominform and Comecon as rivals to the Marshall Plan.
- West Berlin was blockaded by the Soviet Union, Britain and the USA organised a successful airlift to rescue the city.
- The USA agreed to keep their troops in Europe and, with Britain's encouragement, the North Atlantic Treaty Organisation (NATO) was formed.
- The Western-controlled areas of Germany were merged to form Trizonia, which eventually became the Federal Republic of Germany. The Soviet zone became the German Democratic Republic.
- The Soviet Union created a defensive military alliance for the communist countries of Eastern Europe, the Warsaw Pact, in May 1955.

Checkpoint

Strengthen

S1 What was the Truman Doctrine?

S2 What was the role of Comecon?

S3 Describe the events of the Berlin Airlift.

Challenge

C1 How did the Marshall Plan support the ideas of the Truman Doctrine?

C2 Why did Stalin create Cominform and Comecon?

C3 In what way was the USA's signing of the NATO treaty a significant break with the past?

How confident do you feel about your answers to these questions? If you feel unsure, re-read the section then try again.

1.3 The Cold War intensifies

Learning outcomes

- Understand how the arms race between the USA and Soviet Union increased international tension.
- Know about the events of the Hungarian Uprising when the people of Hungary attempted to break free of Soviet rule.

Disagreements over how Germany should be governed had helped divide Europe into two camps by 1949. During the 1950s, tension was further increased as both the USA and the Soviet Union tried to win military supremacy. This resulted in an arms race that led to each side having such powerful weapons that they could destroy their rivals several times over.

The significance of the arms race: Soviet Union *v.* USA, 1950–58

Since developing the atomic bomb in 1945, the USA had felt secure knowing it was the only country in the world with such a powerful weapon. President Truman knew that the atomic bomb was an important counter to the Soviet Union's much larger stocks of conventional* weapons. However, Stalin instructed his scientists to work all-out to develop a Soviet atomic bomb and it was achieved by 1949. In response, the USA developed a hydrogen bomb in 1952. This was 1,000 times more powerful than the atomic bomb and restored the American advantage. One year later, the Soviet Union also had a hydrogen bomb. In 1957, the USA developed the ICBM (inter-continental ballistic missile), which could fire a nuclear warhead at a target more than 4,500 kilometres away. Just a few months later, the Soviet Union was testing its first ICBMs.

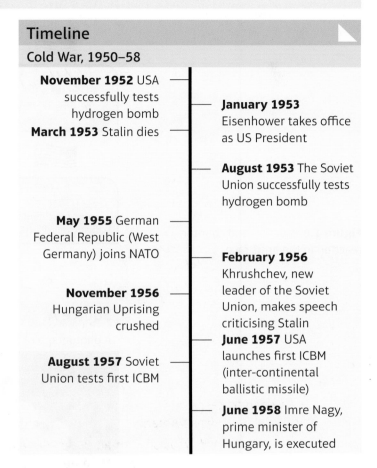

Timeline

Cold War, 1950–58

November 1952 USA successfully tests hydrogen bomb

March 1953 Stalin dies

January 1953 Eisenhower takes office as US President

August 1953 The Soviet Union successfully tests hydrogen bomb

May 1955 German Federal Republic (West Germany) joins NATO

February 1956 Khrushchev, new leader of the Soviet Union, makes speech criticising Stalin

November 1956 Hungarian Uprising crushed

June 1957 USA launches first ICBM (inter-continental ballistic missile)

August 1957 Soviet Union tests first ICBM

June 1958 Imre Nagy, prime minister of Hungary, is executed

Key term

Conventional*

Ordinary or normal. Conventional weapons are defined by the International Committee of the Red Cross as any weapons that are not nuclear, chemical or biological.

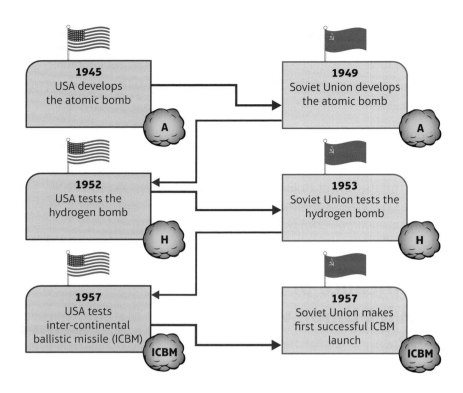

Figure 1.8 Reaction and counter-reaction in the arms race.

Source A

A photograph of a US atom bomb test in the Pacific, in 1951.

The arms race was making each side more powerful, but was it giving either side an advantage? The development of nuclear weapons was typical of what became known as 'the arms race'. Both the USA and the Soviet Union spent huge sums of money on building up large armies, navies, submarine fleets and stocks of conventional and nuclear missiles. It was important to try to stay ahead in the race and stop rivals becoming more powerful. However, the weapons that were being developed were so powerful that, from the early 1950s, both the USA and the Soviet Union could have destroyed the world many times over.

This led to a change in thinking about war. Previously, weapons and armed forces were developed to win wars. Now they were being developed to try and stop the other side from going to war at all. Since both sides understood the risks involved in using nuclear weapons they acted as a deterrent*.

> ### Key term
>
> **Deterrent***
>
> A force that prevents something from happening. In the Cold War, many politicians believed in the 'nuclear deterrent'. They thought a country would be 'deterred' from using nuclear weapons if there was a danger that their enemy would reply with an equally devastating nuclear attack.

New leaders for the USA and the Soviet Union

From 1953, both the USA and the Soviet Union had new leaders. Dwight Eisenhower was elected president of the USA in 1952 and took office in January 1953. His presidential campaign targeted communism and both he and his secretary of state, John Foster Dulles, were strongly anti-communist. Eisenhower was determined to block any attempt at communist expansion, but he was also aware of the dangers posed by nuclear weapons. So he was open to Soviet proposals that there should be talks to improve the relationship between the two superpowers.

Stalin's death on 5 March 1953 led to a power struggle in the Soviet Union, as Stalin had not named a successor. It was not until 1956 that Nikita Khrushchev emerged as the effective ruler of the country. At the Party Congress in that year, he openly criticised Stalin's policies and suggested there should be peaceful co-existence with the West.

Source B

A photograph of Nikita Khrushchev answering questions at a press conference in Paris in 1960.

The change of leadership made people on both sides hopeful that tension between the Soviet Union and USA could be reduced and that a solution to the Cold War arms race could be found. Two other factors contributed to this hope:

- In 1950, there had been a war in Korea in which the USA and Soviet Union supported different sides. But, in July 1953, that war had come to an end.
- Both the USA and the Soviet Union were spending large sums on their armed forces. Both sides knew that reducing spending would be good for their economies.

> ### Extend your knowledge
>
> **The Korean War (1950–53)**
>
> At the end of the Second World War, Korea was split in two. The Soviet Union supported North Korea and the USA supported South Korea. In 1950, North Korea invaded South Korea. The United Nations sent forces to support South Korea, led by the USA. Since the Soviet Union was supporting North Korea, the two superpowers found themselves on opposite sides. They weren't actually fighting each other, but they became involved in bitter diplomatic hostilities.

This new optimism was fuelled by an agreement in 1955 on how Austria should be governed and a summit meeting in Geneva in July 1955. The meeting in Geneva failed to reach agreement over disarmament and the future of Germany, but the atmosphere of co-operation at the meeting reduced some of the tension between East and West.

Unfortunately, the better relations were only short-lived. In May 1955, West Germany joined NATO and the Soviet response was to announce the formation of the Warsaw Pact. So the Geneva meeting took place at a time when suspicion was still growing overall.

The Hungarian Uprising, 1956

During 1956 the people of Hungary began to protest about their lack of political freedoms and problems created by fuel shortages and poor harvests. In October, there were riots in the capital, Budapest, and police clashed with protesters. Soviet troops restored order, but Khrushchev decided to replace Rakosi with Imre Nagy. He was a former prime minister who believed that within a communist regime, there should still be personal freedoms. Khrushchev hoped his appointment would end the protests.

Within days of his appointment Nagy announced a set of proposed reforms. He reorganised the Hungarian government to include members of non-communist parties, ending the one-party state in Hungary. He also authorised the immediate release of many political prisoners and persuaded Khrushchev to withdraw Soviet troops from Hungary. Khrushchev was prepared to accept these reforms if they calmed the unrest in Hungary.

Extend your knowledge

Prime Minister Imre Nagy

Imre Nagy became a communist during the First World War, when he was a prisoner of war in Russia. In 1944, Nagy joined the new communist government in Hungary as minister for agriculture. His support for peasant farmers (rather than the state) got him into trouble and he was expelled from The Communist Party in 1949. After a public statement of loyalty to the Soviet Union Nagy rejoined and even became prime minister (1953–55), but was expelled again in 1955.

Timeline
The Hungarian Uprising, 1956

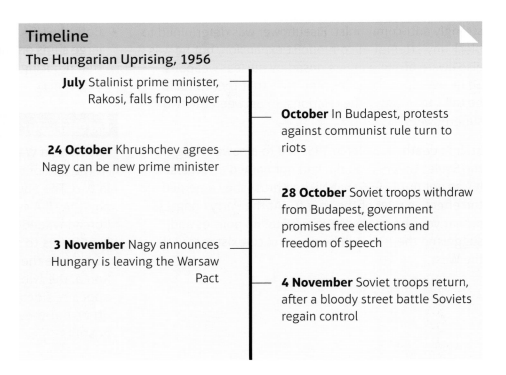

July Stalinist prime minister, Rakosi, falls from power

October In Budapest, protests against communist rule turn to riots

24 October Khrushchev agrees Nagy can be new prime minister

28 October Soviet troops withdraw from Budapest, government promises free elections and freedom of speech

3 November Nagy announces Hungary is leaving the Warsaw Pact

4 November Soviet troops return, after a bloody street battle Soviets regain control

Khrushchev's response to the uprising

However, on 1 November 1956, Nagy announced that Hungary would leave the Warsaw Pact. Khrushchev could not allow this. If Hungary broke away from the Warsaw Pact, other Eastern European countries might follow. Then the whole strategy of achieving security for the Soviet Union by surrounding it with pro-Communist governments would be under threat. Khrushchev therefore ordered a Soviet invasion of Hungary. On 4 November, 1,000 tanks rolled into Budapest. Supporters of Nagy put up a fight in what has become known as the 'Hungarian Uprising' and begged the West for support (see Source C), but no support came. The invading Soviet army acted with great brutality and it is believed that up to 20,000 Hungarians were killed as the Soviet forces re-established control. A new pro-Communist government was set up under Janos Kadar.

Nagy and many of his supporters had believed that Khrushchev's criticism of Stalin would lead to a 'softer' approach with the satellite countries. But they miscalculated. Khrushchev could not allow any threat to Soviet security. Nagy and several members of his cabinet sought refuge in the Yugoslav Embassy. Kadar, promised Nagy that he and his followers could have safe passage out of the country, but when they left the embassy Soviet agents kidnapped them. In July, 1958, the Hungarian Government announced that Nagy had been tried and executed. Khrushchev described his death as 'a lesson to the leaders of all Socialist countries'.

Source C

From a transcript of Imre Nagy's last-minute plea for support as Soviet tanks rolled into Budapest on 4 November 1956.

This fight is the fight for freedom by the Hungarian people against the Russian intervention, and it is possible that I shall only be able to stay at my post for one or two hours. The whole world will see how the Russian armed forces, contrary to all treaties and conventions, are crushing the resistance of the Hungarian people. I should like in these last moments to ask the leaders of the revolution, if they can, to leave the country... [For] today it is Hungary and tomorrow, or the day after tomorrow, it will be the turn of other countries, because the imperialism of Moscow does not know borders and is only trying to play for time.

Extend your knowledge

Polish protests

In the summer of 1956, there were also protests against Soviet control in Poland. Here, the Polish leader, Gomulka, was able to stave off an armed invasion by persuading the Soviets that, while Poland wanted to make some of its own decisions, the Poles were totally loyal to the Warsaw Pact and to communism.

Source D

A photograph of Hungarian rebels waving their national flag in Budapest, Hungary. They are standing on top of a captured Soviet tank.

International reaction to the Soviet invasion of Hungary

When Nagy had proposed leaving the Warsaw Pact, he and his fellow rebels expected support from the USA and other Western nations. Radio Free Europe, a US government-funded radio station, regularly broadcast messages urging the people of Eastern Europe to rise up against the communist regime. Since the US had offered financial aid through the Marshall Plan, people in Eastern Europe assumed they would be ready to help in other ways.

Eisenhower was sympathetic to the Hungarians, and some NATO nations in Europe did take in Hungarian refugees, but no military support was offered to the Hungarians during the uprising. The US policy of containment meant that while there might be a situation where the USA would take military action to prevent the Soviet Union spreading communism beyond the satellite states, it was not prepared to interfere in the affairs of an existing communist country. A military attack on a Soviet satellite state could trigger nuclear war. This would result in the destruction of both sides – a far worse result than leaving rebels to fight the Soviets alone.

What was the impact of the Hungarian Uprising on international relations?

The Hungarian Uprising made Khrushchev's position in the Soviet Union much more secure and gave him a stronger position in the Warsaw Pact. Members knew they must do as they were told. If they rebelled they could not expect military support from the USA. Khrushchev also became more confident in dealing with the USA because he now knew they were unlikely to risk taking military action.

In some ways, the failure of the Hungarian Uprising reflected badly on the West. The USA and its allies had encouraged communist countries to stand up to the Soviet Union, but were not prepared to back up their words with military support.

Even though the USA did not take military action, it strongly opposed the Soviet invasion of Hungary, and Khrushchev's crackdown soured relations between the two superpowers once more.

Friendlier relations at the Geneva Summit had looked like a thaw in the Cold War, but it was short-lived and the events of the 1960s (covered in Chapter 2) would make the Cold War even 'colder'.

Activities ?

1   You are a military adviser to President Eisenhower. He asks for a summary of reasons why he should support the Hungarian Uprising. What do you say?

2   President Eisenhower says he has received a report from another adviser with reasons why the USA should not intervene in Hungary. What do you think the report says?

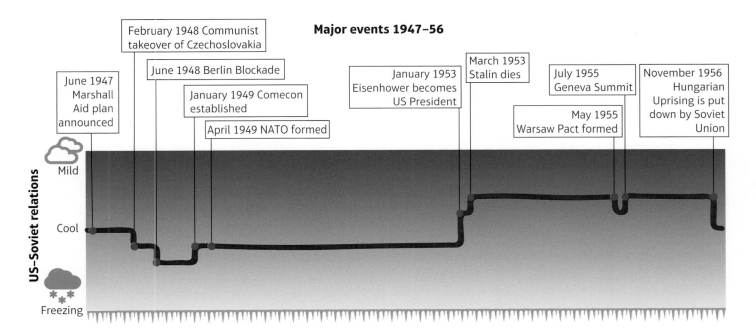

Figure 1.9 Tensions between the USA and the Soviet Union, 1946–58.

Summary

- In the 1950s, the arms race between the USA and the Soviet Union accelerated, with a massive build-up of nuclear arms on both sides. Both sides had enough weapons to destroy each other and the world several times over.
- In 1953, the election of Eisenhower and the death of Stalin seemed to reduce tension in the Cold War.
- When West Germany joined NATO, the Soviets set up the Warsaw Pact.
- A rebellion against Soviet domination of Hungary in 1956 was put down with armed force. The Hungarian Uprising did serious damage to East–West relations.

Checkpoint

Strengthen

S1 What new types of weapons were developed in the 1950s?

S2 What is meant by 'deterrence' in the Cold War?

S3 When did West Germany join NATO?

Challenge

C1 Why did people think there might be an end to the Cold War after Stalin died?

C2 If both the USA and the Soviet Union already had the capability to destroy their rivals by 1950, why did they keep creating new weapons?

C3 Why did Hungarians think their uprising would receive outside support?

How confident do you feel about your answers to these questions? If you're not sure you answered them well, form a group with other students, discuss the answers and then record your conclusions. Your teacher can give you some hints.

Recap: The origins of the Cold War, 1941–58

Recall quiz

1 Which countries were members of The Grand Alliance?

2 What years were the conferences at Tehran, Yalta and Potsdam held?

3 Who were the leaders of The Grand Alliance up to 1945? Who were the new leaders in that year?

4 What was the Truman Doctrine?

5 Explain what a 'satellite state' is.

6 Which countries joined NATO?

7 Which countries joined the Warsaw Pact?

8 In what year was West Germany created?

9 What is an ICBM?

10 Who was leader of the Soviet Union during the Hungarian Uprising?

Exam-style question, Section A

Explain **two** consequences of the Hungarian Uprising in 1956. **8 marks**

Exam tip

Remember this question is about consequences, not events. So don't spend time saying what happened during the uprising. Focus on explaining what happened as a result of the uprising.

Activity ?

Copy the table below, but give it ten rows. Pick ten events between 1941 and 1958 and complete the columns to show their impact on relations between East and West. The first one is done for you.

Event	Brief summary	Did it improve or harm relations
Formation of The Grand Alliance	USA, the Soviet Union and Britain join to fight Hitler	Improved

1 Write a short paragraph explaining why Britain, the Soviet Union and the USA were allies until 1945. Why was the alliance difficult? Why did it end in 1945?

2 Explain why Germany was divided into two parts, including as many reasons as you can.

3 With a partner discuss how far you agree with the following statement: 'Relations between East and West were far worse in 1958 than they were at the end of the Second World War'.

Writing historically: building information

When you are asked to write an explanation or analysis, you need to provide as much detailed information as possible.

Learning objectives

By the end of this lesson you will understand how to:

- add clear and detailed information to your writing by using relative clauses and noun phrases in apposition.

Definitions

Relative clause: a clause which adds information or **modifies** a noun, linked with a **relative pronoun**, for example: *who, that, which, where, whose*.

Noun in apposition: two **noun phrases**, positioned side-by-side, the second adding information to the first, for example: [1] Budapest, [2] the capital of Hungary, was the scene of mass protests.

How can I add detail to my writing?

Look at a sentence from the response below to this exam-style question.

> Explain **two** consequences of the decisions made by The Grand Alliance at the Yalta Conference in February 1945.　　**(8 marks)**

> Britain and the USA supported the 'London Poles', who were non-Communists.

The main clause is highlighted in yellow. The relative pronoun is highlighted in green. The relative clause is highlighted in purple.

This noun phrase is modified by this relative clause: it provides more information about the London Poles.

   1. How could you restructure the sentence above using two separate sentences?

   2. Why do you think the writers chose to structure these sentences using a main clause and a relative clause instead of writing them as two separate sentences?

Now look at these four sentences taken from the same response:

> The Soviet Union and the USA failed to come to an agreement on how to govern Poland. Both countries thought there should be free elections. Stalin thought elections should lead to a pro-communist government. The US government supported the 'London Poles'.

   3. How effectively is this information expressed? Write a sentence or two explaining your answer.

   4. How could you improve the written expression in the answer above, using relative pronouns?

     a. Rewrite the sentences, using relative pronouns to link all the information in **one** sentence.

     b. Now rewrite the sentence using relative pronouns to link the information in **two** sentences.

     c. Which version do you prefer? Is the information most clearly and fluently expressed in one, two or four sentences? Write a sentence or two explaining your choice.

How can I add detail to my writing in different ways?

You can also add detail to a sentence using a **noun phrase in apposition**.

Compare these sentences:

> The leaders of the Soviet Union and USA, who were called Stalin and Truman, began to distrust each other.

This writer has used a relative clause to add information clearly and succinctly.

> The leaders of the Soviet Union and USA, Stalin and Truman, began to distrust each other.

This writer has used a noun phrase in apposition to add the same information clearly and succinctly.

> **5.** How could you combine the information in these pairs of sentences using a noun phrase in apposition?

> Stalin was highly suspicious of Germany. He wanted Poland to form a buffer zone between Germany and the Soviet Union's Western border.
>
> Stalin wanted a Communist government in Poland. This was part of his plan to make Poland into a buffer zone protecting the Soviet Union.

Did you notice?

> **6.** If you remove the relative clause or the noun phrase in apposition from the two sentences at the top of the page, they both still make sense. They are also both separated from the rest of the sentence with commas. Can you explain why? Write a sentence or two explaining your ideas.

Improving an answer

> **7.** Look at an extract from another response to the exam question on the previous page.

> The Yalta conference was held in February 1945. The conference led to an increase in suspicion between Stalin and the USA. The increase in suspicion was due to failure to agree on how Poland should be governed. The superpowers did agree that there should be an election to choose a new government for Poland. Stalin planned to influence the elections. He wanted a pro-Moscow government to be elected. The USA supported free elections and wanted the London Poles to win the elections.

> **a.** Rewrite the information in the answer above, making it as clear and succinct as possible. You could use:
>
>   • relative clauses
>
>   • nouns in apposition.

> **b.** Look carefully at your response to question 7a. Are all your sentences easy to read and understand, or are some of them too long and confusing? If so, try rewriting them to make their meaning as clear as possible.

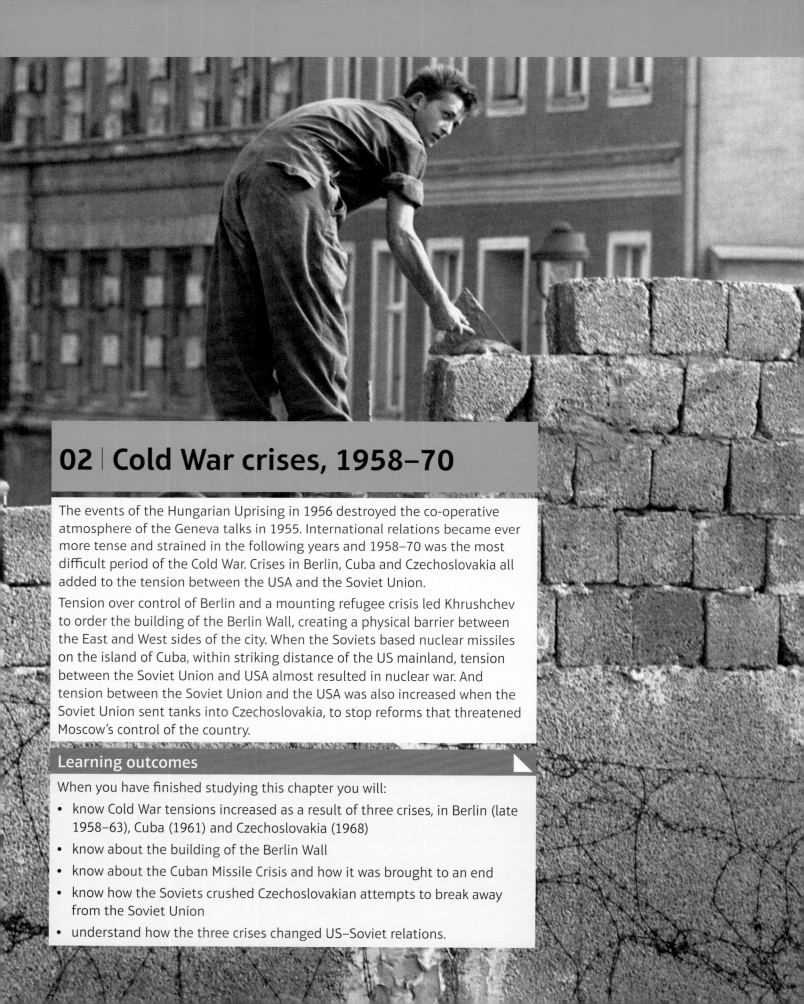

02 | Cold War crises, 1958–70

The events of the Hungarian Uprising in 1956 destroyed the co-operative atmosphere of the Geneva talks in 1955. International relations became ever more tense and strained in the following years and 1958–70 was the most difficult period of the Cold War. Crises in Berlin, Cuba and Czechoslovakia all added to the tension between the USA and the Soviet Union.

Tension over control of Berlin and a mounting refugee crisis led Khrushchev to order the building of the Berlin Wall, creating a physical barrier between the East and West sides of the city. When the Soviets based nuclear missiles on the island of Cuba, within striking distance of the US mainland, tension between the Soviet Union and USA almost resulted in nuclear war. And tension between the Soviet Union and the USA was also increased when the Soviet Union sent tanks into Czechoslovakia, to stop reforms that threatened Moscow's control of the country.

Learning outcomes

When you have finished studying this chapter you will:

- know Cold War tensions increased as a result of three crises, in Berlin (late 1958–63), Cuba (1961) and Czechoslovakia (1968)
- know about the building of the Berlin Wall
- know about the Cuban Missile Crisis and how it was brought to an end
- know how the Soviets crushed Czechoslovakian attempts to break away from the Soviet Union
- understand how the three crises changed US–Soviet relations.

2.1 Berlin 1958–63: Increased tension and the impact of the Berlin Wall

Learning outcomes

- Understand why there was a crisis in Berlin, 1958–61.
- Know how Khrushchev tried to deal with the refugee problem and how Kennedy reacted.
- Understand how the Berlin Crisis affected international relations.

Timeline

Berlin Crisis, 1958–61

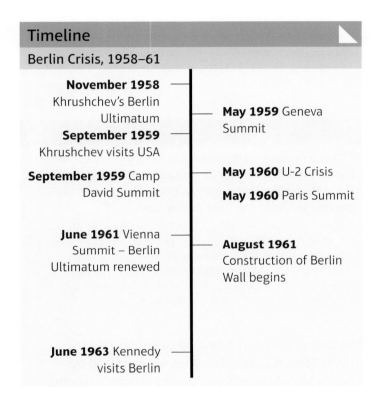

November 1958
Khrushchev's Berlin Ultimatum

May 1959 Geneva Summit

September 1959
Khrushchev visits USA

September 1959 Camp David Summit

May 1960 U-2 Crisis

May 1960 Paris Summit

June 1961 Vienna Summit – Berlin Ultimatum renewed

August 1961
Construction of Berlin Wall begins

June 1963 Kennedy visits Berlin

were constantly monitored by the secret police. In 1953, there were riots against the government and the Soviet government sent an armed force to restore order.

Under these circumstances, it is not surprising that many East Germans chose to leave home and move to West Germany. They knew that the quality of life in West Germany was much higher and it was easy to cross the border. All they had to do was travel from East to West Berlin. Once there, they could freely travel to other parts of the country.

By 1958, three million East Germans, over a sixth of the country's population, had crossed to the West. Many of them were exactly the kind of people East Germany urgently needed to build its economy. Skilled workers, such as engineers, technicians and teachers left, knowing that they could earn much higher salaries in West Germany.

The refugee problem in Berlin, 1958

In 1949, Germany had been divided into two: West Germany was democratic and East Germany was firmly under the control of the communist Soviet Union. West Germany received Marshall Aid and during the 1950s became a prosperous country where most people enjoyed a high standard of living. East Germany received far less aid from the Soviet Union and the government's economic policies in the 1950s were largely unsuccessful, so East Germans suffered from a low standard of living and shortages of basic goods. The communist regime in East Germany was increasingly unpopular. There were many restrictions on what ordinary citizens could say and do and they

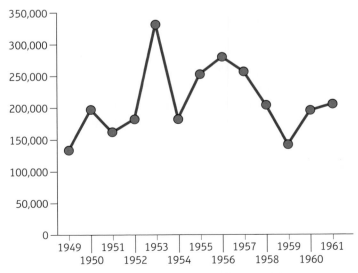

Figure 2.1 Numbers of refugees crossing from East to West Germany, 1949–61.

The Soviet leader, Khrushchev, could not allow this situation to continue. Not only was East Germany losing valuable people, but communism was facing a propaganda disaster. In Berlin, people had a choice between the communist East and the capitalist West. They were making it clear that they preferred the West.

Khrushchev's Berlin ultimatum

Khrushchev decided the answer was for the whole of Berlin to become part of the surrounding territory of East Germany. If the Americans, British and French left Berlin, it would be much harder for East Germans to get into West Germany. But Khrushchev knew that Britain, France and the USA would not agree to leave. They would have to be forced.

So in November 1958, Khrushchev demanded that Western countries should officially recognise East Germany as an independent country. Because they still believed that Germany could be reunited they refused to do so.

On 27 November, Khrushchev issued his Berlin Ultimatum*. He demanded that:

- Berlin should be demilitarised and Western troops withdrawn
- Berlin should became a free city*.

The West had six months to make these changes or Khrushchev would hand over control of all routes into Berlin to the government of East Germany.

Khrushchev's threat to hand over control of transport to the East Berlin government was a clever move. If this happened, it would force the Western powers to talk to the East German authorities and so force them to acknowledge East Germany was a legitimate country.

Key terms

Ultimatum*

A final demand, often backed up with a threat to take action.

Free city*

A city with its own independent government. Khrushchev did not really mean to make Berlin independent – he wanted it to be controlled by the Soviet Union.

Source A

Extract from Nikita Khrushchev's speech about Berlin, given on 10 November 1958.

The time has obviously arrived for the signatories of the Potsdam Agreement to renounce the remnants of the occupation regime in Berlin and thereby make it possible to create a normal situation in the capital of the German Democratic Republic. The Soviet Union, for its part, would hand over to the sovereign German Democratic Republic the functions in Berlin that are still exercised by Soviet agencies. This, I think, would be the correct thing to do.

Source B

This is an extract from a note sent from the Soviet Foreign Ministry to the American Ambassador at Moscow. It was titled 'Regarding Berlin' and sent on 27 November 1958. It became known as the Berlin Ultimatum.

If the statesmen responsible for the policy of the Western powers are guided by feelings of hatred for communism and the socialist countries in their approach to the Berlin question as well as other international problems, no good will come out of it.

The Berlin Ultimatum had a major impact on international relations. The West was outraged by Khrushchev's demands and saw his actions as another example of the Soviet Union trying to spread communism. Khrushchev, however, saw his demands as essential action to stop the flood of skilled citizens from East Germany.

By 1958, both the USA and the Soviet Union had large numbers of nuclear weapons and neither side wanted this crisis to lead to war. Even the West German Chancellor, Adenauer, who was fiercely opposed to giving East Germany official recognition and believed West Germany was the only 'real' Germany, was not prepared to go to war over the issue of Berlin. So between 1959 and 1961, a series of talks were held to try to solve the 'Berlin problem'.

The summit meetings of 1959–61

Geneva, May 1959

The first summit meeting between the foreign ministers of the various countries was held in Geneva, in neutral Switzerland. Both sides put forward proposals for how Berlin should be governed, but no agreement was reached. President Eisenhower invited Khrushchev to the USA for further talks.

Camp David, September 1959

Eisenhower and Khrushchev met face-to-face for the first time at the presidential ranch. There was still no agreement about a way forward for Berlin but the Soviets did agree to withdraw the Berlin Ultimatum. The meeting appeared to establish better relations between the two leaders and it was agreed that further talks would be held in Paris the following summer.

Extend your knowledge

Khrushchev in the USA

In 1959, Khrushchev made the first ever visit by a Soviet leader to the USA. He ate hot dogs, met ordinary people, visited Hollywood and seemed to enjoy himself. However, after a meeting between Khrushchev and Eisenhower, the American president was not convinced that the Soviet policy on Berlin had actually changed.

Paris, May 1960

As the various parties prepared for the Paris talks, the Soviet Union made an announcement that destroyed any chance of those talks being successful. On 1 May, they had shot down an American U-2 spy-plane as it flew over the Soviet Union. The Americans tried to claim it was a weather plane that had blown off-course, but the Soviets interrogated the pilot, Gary Powers, who admitted to being on a spying mission. Although President Eisenhower was embarrassed by what had happened, he refused to apologise, saying that spying operations like this were unavoidable. Khrushchev walked out of the meeting and it ended with no decisions being made.

Source C

A photograph of Soviet people looking at the remains of the U-2 spy-plane shot down over the Soviet Union in May 1960.

Interpretation 1

A recent account of the Paris Summit and U-2 incident from the *US Department of State Official History* website.

Khrushchev had publicly committed himself to the idea of "peaceful coexistence" with the United States... [Had] the United States apologized, he would have continued the summit. Eisenhower, however, refused to issue a formal apology... . On May 11, Eisenhower finally acknowledged his full awareness of the entire program and of the Powers flight in particular. Moreover, he explained that... such spy flights were a necessary element in maintaining national defense, and that he planned to continue them.

Extend your knowledge

US spy-planes

During the Cold War, the US Air Force (USAF) and the Central Intelligence Agency (CIA) used U-2 jet-engine planes to fly spy missions over enemy countries. Many flew over the Soviet Union, often from USAF bases in friendly nations such as Pakistan.

Vienna, June 1961

In January 1961, John F. Kennedy became president of the USA. Kennedy followed a policy of building up the USA's military forces, but at the same time trying to resolve difficulties with the Soviet Union through talks.

Khrushchev believed that as Kennedy was inexperienced in foreign affairs, it would be possible to get the better of him. He also knew that Kennedy's reputation had suffered when an American invasion of Cuba at the 'Bay of Pigs' in April 1961 failed (see page 50). So, at a new round of talks held in Vienna in June 1961, Khrushchev took a tough stance and renewed the Berlin Ultimatum of 1958.

Kennedy was extremely concerned by Khrushchev's approach, but was determined not to appear weak and not to give way over control of Berlin. He refused to make any concessions and once again the meeting ended with no final decision on Berlin. The personal relationship between Kennedy and Khrushchev became very strained.

After Vienna, Kennedy decided to increase spending on American armed forces by over $2 billion to protect the USA if war broke out. It seemed that, if necessary, the USA was prepared to fight over Berlin.

Source D

President Kennedy speaking to the American people after his return from the Vienna Summit in 1961.

We do not want to fight — but we have fought before. And others in earlier times have made the same dangerous mistake of assuming that the West was too selfish and too soft and too divided to resist invasions of freedom in other lands... . We cannot and will not permit the Communists to drive us out of Berlin, either gradually or by force... . Our pledge to that city is essential to the morale and security of Western Germany, to the unity of Western Europe, and to the faith of the entire Free World.

Extend your knowledge

President John F. Kennedy

John Fitzgerald Kennedy was one of the youngest men ever to be elected President of the United States, he took office aged just 43. Born in 1917, he came from a very wealthy family. He fought in the Second World War and served as a Senator before becoming President. Many, like Khrushchev, saw Kennedy as an inexperienced youth, whose wealth gave him no understanding of the real world. Events in Berlin and Cuba proved Khrushchev's assumptions were wrong.

Activities ?

1   Write a paragraph summarising the results of each summit held between 1959 and 1961.

2   For each summit, highlight what went well and what went wrong. In a small group, discuss what made some summits more successful than others and what would have made the talks more successful.

3   'In reality, the summits were a complete waste of time'. How far do you agree with this statement? Write a short paragraph to explain your answer.

Building the Berlin Wall

Khrushchev's tough line on Berlin had forced Britain, France and the USA to get involved in talks about the city's future. However, it had an unfortunate side-effect. As tension between East and West grew, so more East Germans decided to cross to the West, just in case Khrushchev decided to close the border. On just one day in August 1961, for example, 40,000 East Germans crossed to the West.

The East German leader, Walter Ulbricht, urged Khrushchev to close the border. So on the night of 12 August 1961, East German troops built a barbed wire fence around Berlin and between East and West Berlin.

This was only the beginning. Soon work on a concrete wall, which would stretch 165 kilometres, began. It seemed that discussions were over. Berlin and Germany were to stay split in two and East Germany's refugee problem was solved.

Impacts of the Berlin Wall

The impact in Berlin

The Berlin Wall cut through streets and even buildings. While it was being built, many more people made escape attempts. One woman threw a mattress out of the window into West Berlin and then jumped onto it. She landed on the mattress but later died of her injuries. The West Berlin fire service tried to help others ready to jump by catching them in blankets.

By the end of the summer, the wall was finished. Along the 27-mile section that cut through the centre of Berlin there were (strictly speaking) two walls, one facing East, and the other West. They were separated by a zone known as 'no-man's land' packed with booby-traps, barbed wire, minefields and car-barriers, all guarded by hundreds of lookout towers, with machine-gun nests and powerful searchlights. Families, friends and neighbours were parted, often for years on end.

Source E

No-man's land between East and West Berlin.

In desperation, some people tried to cross the Wall. East German border guards were instructed to shoot anyone making the attempt and it is estimated that over 130 people were killed. One of the saddest failed attempts to cross the Berlin Wall came in August 1962, when two building workers made a dash for it. One reached West Berlin, but the other, Peter Fechter, was shot. He fell back into East Berlin and lay dying for 45 minutes. As thousands of West Germans yelled 'murderers' across the border, East German guards eventually took the body away.

Source F

The body of Peter Fechter is carried away by East German border guards after he was shot attempting to cross the Berlin Wall into West Berlin in 1962.

Activities

1   Look at Source E. Why do you think no one tried to rescue Peter Fechter?

2   In small groups, choose one of the following roles and prepare a 30-second speech to convince the rest of your class.

   a   President Kennedy saying why Khrushchev was wrong to build the Wall

   b   Khrushchev explaining why he was right to build the Wall.

3   Which of these views do you think the people of Berlin would have agreed with? Explain why you think this.

Impact of the wall on the USA and Soviet Union

The building of the Berlin Wall had positive and negative results for the USA and Soviet Union.

	Negative outcomes	Positive outcomes
Soviet Union	Khrushchev had to abandon plans to unite Germany under Soviet control. The Wall showed that the Soviet Union had to 'lock' people into East Germany to stop them leaving. Given a choice, they seemed to prefer capitalism over communism.	The Wall stopped refugees leaving for the West through East Berlin. The Wall sent the West a message that communism would survive in Berlin, and that any attempt to reunite Germany under Western control would fail.
USA	The Soviet Union had closed the border without consulting the USA. Those people who wanted to escape from communism were no longer able to.	The Wall showed that Khrushchev had been forced to accept Western control in West Berlin, and that did not think he could get away with bullying Kennedy anymore. West Berlin became an emblem of freedom and defiance against communism.

The positive results for Kennedy's reputation were demonstrated when he visited West Berlin in 1963. Thousands of West Berliners turned out to see him. He was treated like a rock star or sporting hero – his route was showered with flowers, rice and shredded paper and crowds chanted his name.

West Berliners were celebrating their freedom in contrast to the restrictions of life in the East as well as the arrival of a famous visitor. During the visit, Kennedy praised the freedoms of the West and contrasted them with communism in a famous speech in which he said, '*Ich bin ein Berliner*.' ('I am a citizen of Berlin.')

Source H

John F. Kennedy giving the '*Ich bin ein Berliner*' speech, on 26 June 1963.

Source G

From a speech given by Kennedy on 26 June 1963. The speech was given in a public square in Berlin.

Two thousand years ago the proudest boast was '*civis Romanus sum*' [I am a Roman citizen]. Today, in the world of freedom, the proudest boast is '*Ich bin ein Berliner*' [I am a citizen of Berlin].

There are many people in the world who really don't understand, or say they don't, what is the great issue between the free world and the Communist world. Let them come to Berlin.

There are some who say that Communism is the future. Let them come to Berlin.

And there are some who say in Europe and elsewhere we can work with the Communists. Let them come to Berlin.

And there are even a few who say that it is true that Communism is an evil system, but it permits us to make economic progress. *Lass' sie nach Berlin kommen*. Let them come to Berlin.

Extend your knowledge

'*Ich bin ein Berliner*'

In Kennedy's 1963 speech in Berlin, he said '*Ich bin ein Berliner*'. 'Berliner' means 'citizen of Berlin' but also 'doughnut' – so some people have argued that Kennedy literally said 'I am a doughnut'! The crowd in Berlin doesn't seem to have thought this, or cared if that was what he said. They loved Kennedy's message and the fact that he tried to say it in German.

Impacts on international relations

Although the building of the Wall led to increased tension between the Soviet Union and USA, there were also positive results.

Negative outcomes	Positive outcomes
The two sides had been arguing about Germany since the Second World War. Numerous meetings and summits had failed to resolve the issue. Now things were so bad that the Soviets had built a concrete wall dividing Germany. This reminded people of Churchill's 1946 speech in which he spoke of an 'Iron Curtain' (see page 16).	Now Berlin was divided and the borders between East and West Germany were closed; there was less likelihood that the US and Soviet Union would go to war over Berlin. The Americans complained bitterly about the building of the Wall, but as Kennedy said, a wall was better than war.
The Berlin Wall became a powerful symbol of the differences between East and West for almost 30 years, until it was taken down in 1989.	So, in some ways, the building of the Wall may have reduced tension between the USA and the Soviet Union.

However, any improvement in relations was soon destroyed by events in Cuba in 1962.

Exam-style question, Section A

Write a narrative account analysing the key events of the 'Berlin Crisis' in the years 1958–61.

You may use the following in your answer:

- the Berlin Ultimatum, 1958
- the construction of the Berlin Wall.

You **must** also use information of your own. **8 marks**

Exam tip

Remember that the key to scoring well on this type of question is to create a coherent narrative that links together events and explains how one leads to the next in a logical and structured way.

Summary

- Khrushchev was worried about East German citizens crossing into West Germany.
- Talks between the USA and the Soviet Union about Berlin broke down.
- Khrushchev decided to build the Berlin Wall.
- Kennedy visited West Berlin to show his support.
- The Berlin Wall now acted as a symbol of the division of Europe.

Checkpoint

Strengthen

S1 What was Khrushchev's Berlin Ultimatum?

S2 Why did he issue this ultimatum?

S3 Why did the Paris Summit in 1960 fail?

Challenge

C1 After the summit meetings of 1959–61, do you think Khrushchev would have thought Kennedy was a stronger or weaker leader than he had previously thought?

C2 Berlin is thousands of kilometres from the USA, so why did Kennedy care what happened to it?

C3 In what way could the building of the Berlin Wall have helped relations between the USA and the Soviet Union?

How confident do you feel about your answers to these questions? Form a small group and discuss any questions you are not sure about. Look for the answers in this section. Now rewrite your answers together in your group.

Learning outcomes

- Understand why Cuba became a threat to the USA.
- Know how Kennedy dealt with Khrushchev's attempt to put nuclear missiles on Cuba.
- Understand how the crisis affected international relations.

The Cuban Revolution

In January 1959, a group of revolutionaries, led by Fidel Castro and Che Guevara, toppled the pro-American government of Cuba. President Eisenhower was concerned about the revolution as there were very close links between Cuba and the USA. American businesses had invested heavily in Cuba and much of the land was owned by Americans. Cuba's oil refineries, electricity and phone networks and railways were also controlled by Americans and the USA was an important investor in Cuba's main export, sugar. The new leader of Cuba, Fidel Castro, was a nationalist who did not want his country's economy to be under American control. This created tension between the USA and Cuba, which grew into a crisis threatening world peace.

In the aftermath of the revolution, there were three main areas of tension:

- The American government reluctantly recognised the new government, but refused to provide economic aid unless Cuba followed guidelines set out by the International Monetary Fund.
- In May 1959, the Cuban government took over all land in Cuba owned by foreign nationals. It paid compensation to previous owners, but the US government refused to recognise the scheme. Castro took the land anyway.
- Castro had already begun appointing communists to his government when, in February 1960, he made an agreement with the Soviet Union. Khrushchev agreed to buy Cuban sugar and provide economic aid. There was also a secret clause saying that Cuba would receive arms from the Soviet Union.

Timeline

Cuban Revolution and the Cuban Missile Crisis, 1959–63

January 1959 Castro becomes leader of Cuba

May 1959 Cuban government nationalises foreign-owned land in Cuba

February 1960 Castro signs agreement with Khrushchev

January 1961 USA breaks off diplomatic relations with Cuba

August 1961 'Bay of Pigs' invasion

September 1961 Khrushchev offers weapons to Cuba

14 October 1962 U-2 spy-plane pictures show Soviet missile silos

16 October 1962 Kennedy assembles advisory group ExComm, beginning of 'Thirteen Days'

June 1963 Telephone 'hotline' set up

August 1963 Test Ban treaty

22 October 1962 Kennedy appears on national television to announce blockade

28 October 1962 Soviet Union agrees to remove nuclear missiles from Cuba

Source A

Fidel Castro and Nikita Khrushchev meet at the United Nations in New York, in 1960.

The USA was extremely concerned that a pro-Soviet regime was being established just 145 kilometres from the US mainland and decided to take action to try to bring Cuba into line. In July 1960, Eisenhower reduced the amount of sugar the USA would buy from Cuba and in October banned all trade with the country. In January 1961, the USA broke off diplomatic relations with Cuba.

The USA intervenes in Cuba: the 'Bay of Pigs' incident

President Kennedy (who took over from Eisenhower in 1961) did not want a Communist ally so close to American territory. He therefore gave his support to a plan agreed by the Central Intelligence Agency (CIA) and Eisenhower before he was elected. The CIA suggested that a group of Cuban exiles could be trained to launch an invasion and overthrow Castro. Sending Cuban exiles would make the attack look like a Cuban counter-revolution, so the USA could claim not to have been involved.

On 17 April 1961, an invasion force of around 1,400 Cuban exiles landed at the 'Bay of Pigs' in Cuba.

The USA hoped they would topple the Castro regime and put a new US-friendly government in control of the island. The attempted coup was a complete failure, for several reasons:

- The volunteers had little military experience. They received some training from the CIA, but they were no match for the battle-hardened Cuban revolutionary army.
- The USA wanted to present the attack as a Cuban effort to get rid of Castro. As a result, they could not send US ground forces or air strikes to support the attack.
- Castro's government found out about the invasion plans. There were 20,000 soldiers ready and waiting to fight off 1,400 invaders.
- The USA and the exile army wrongly assumed that most Cubans would support them. But many ordinary Cubans felt happy with Castro and did not rush to lend their support.

Castro showed wrecked aeroplanes and other evidence of the Cuban victory to journalists from around the world. The American involvement was undeniable and the defeat became a public humiliation for the USA.

Source B

Anti-Castro fighters captured during the 'Bay of Pigs' operation.

Effects of the 'Bay of Pigs' incident on international relations

The 'Bay of Pigs' was a humiliating and embarrassing failure for the United States. The USA had previously accused the Soviet Union of trying to build an empire in Eastern Europe. Now it looked like the Americans were acting in exactly the same way to restore American influence in an independent country by supporting an armed uprising against its government.

The Soviet Union was quick to point out that the people of Cuba were happy under the leadership of the pro-communist Castro and had shown little support for the Cuban exiles' attempt to restore the pro-American and corrupt Batista regime. Khrushchev said this was a clear indication of the popularity of communism.

The 'Bay of Pigs' incident inevitably led to stronger relations between Cuba and the Soviet Union. After defeating the invasion, Castro declared himself to be a communist and asked Khrushchev to help him defend Cuba against any future attack from the USA. In September 1961, Khrushchev publicly announced that he would provide arms to Cuba.

President Kennedy was extremely concerned by this. Cuba would now have modern military equipment and training from Soviet experts.

If the Soviet Union placed nuclear weapons on Cuba, the USA would be under direct threat. Kennedy warned Khrushchev that he could not allow the Soviet Union to use Cuba as a base to threaten the USA. Khrushchev assured him that he had no intention of doing so, but the Americans were soon to discover that this was not the case.

Source C

Extracts from a 1961 US government inquiry into the 'Bay of Pigs' operation.

Scrutiny of the plans for the operation would have shown that Castro's ability to fight back and roll up internal opposition needed to be taken more seriously... . Why did the United States contemplate pitting 1,500 soldiers, however well-trained and armed, against an enemy vastly superior in number and arms. We can confidently assert that the CIA had no evidence that Cubans in significant numbers would join the invaders... . The project has lost all elements of secrecy as for more than 3 months the American press had been reporting on the recruitment and training of Cubans. The CIA's name was freely linked with these activities. Denial was a pathetic illusion.

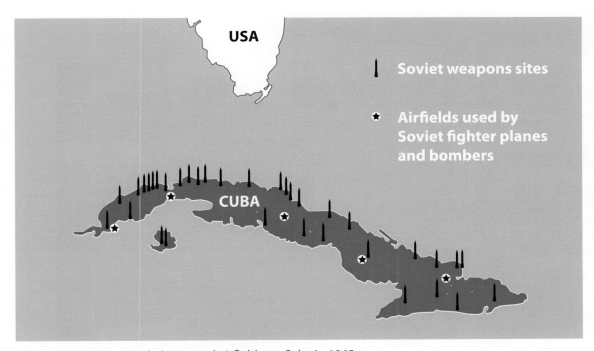

Figure 2.2 Soviet missile bases and airfields on Cuba in 1962.

Activities ?

1. Why was the USA concerned about Castro's take-over in Cuba?

2. Explain the American thinking behind the 'Bay of Pigs' invasion.

3. Broadcasters love to hear 'soundbites'. In Source C, 'Denial was a pathetic illusion' is an excellent 'soundbite'. Working with a partner:

   a. in as few words as possible explain what the soundbite means

   b. summarise what the report says went wrong with the invasion.

The Cuban Missile Crisis

On 14 October 1962, an America U-2 spy-plane took pictures of what seemed to be launch pads for medium-range ballistic missiles, which could carry nuclear warheads capable of causing terrible damage to US cities. American intelligence agencies informed President Kennedy that a fleet of Soviet ships was sailing to Cuba, presumably carrying the missiles themselves.

Khrushchev had previously told Kennedy that he would not put nuclear weapons on Cuba. Why did he now take this highly provocative step? There were several reasons.

- In Europe, NATO had missiles based in Turkey, just a short distance from the Soviet Union. Khrushchev believed it was time for the USA to feel what it was like to be under threat. It was also possible that Khrushchev's real aim was to have the missiles in Turkey removed.
- The building of the Berlin Wall was portrayed by many Soviet critics as a failure for Khrushchev. If he could outwit Kennedy over Cuba, it would restore his prestige.
- Khrushchev may also have wanted to put missiles in Cuba because he feared another American attack. If the Americans overthrew Castro, this would be seen as another defeat for communism.

Source D

This photo, taken on 23 October 1962 by an American U-2 spy-plane, showed that further work had been done on the missile launch site in Cuba since it was originally spotted on 14 October.

The Soviet Union could have fired nuclear missiles at the USA from their own territory, so siting missiles on Cuba did not make a great deal of practical difference. But it made a huge political difference. As far as Kennedy was concerned, the Soviet Union had to be stopped from siting nuclear missiles on Cuba, for many reasons. The question was how could he take action without triggering a full-blown war? Defense Secretary Robert McNamara advised that the missiles could become operational in two weeks. There was no time to waste.

Figure 2.3 Kennedy's options at the time of the Cuban Missile Crisis.

Source E

An extract from a statement made by Dean Acheson, one of Kennedy's advisers, at a meeting held on 17 October 1962 to discuss what action the USA should take over Cuba.

We should proceed at once with the necessary military action and do no talking. The Soviets will react someplace. We must expect this, take the consequences and manage the situations as they evolve. We should have no consultations with Khrushchev, Castro or our allies, though we should alert our allies.

Activities ?

1 Khrushchev must have known that the USA would object to Soviet nuclear missiles being placed in Cuba. Suggest reasons why this did not stop him from doing so.

2 Look at Source E.

   a Summarise Acheson's point-of-view in one sentence.

   b Acheson's position could well have led to war. Does that mean the USA was prepared to fight the Soviet Union?

Key term

Hawks*

During the Cold War, those who supported going to war were known as Hawks. Their counterparts, who tried to find solutions to problems without going to war, were known as Doves.

The Thirteen Days, 16–28 October 1962

On 16 October, Kennedy called together an Executive Committee (ExComm for short) to discuss how the USA should react. ExComm met every day for thirteen days, during which the world faced the threat of nuclear war.

After several days of discussion, on 22 October, Kennedy decided not to launch an attack. Instead he set up a naval blockade around Cuba. No ships would be allowed to pass through the blockade without US permission. Kennedy appeared on US television that evening to inform a shocked US public about the missiles in Cuba. Many Americans expected the Soviet Union to ignore the blockade. Then the USA would have to sink their ships and war would follow. Kennedy was aware of this and prepared 54 bombers, each with four nuclear warheads, in case war broke out. The world held its breath.

On 24 October, the Soviet ships reached the blockade – and turned around! Dean Rusk, the US Secretary of State, told Kennedy, 'I think the other guy just blinked!'

From confrontation to agreement

The Soviet decision not to break through the naval blockade meant direct confrontation had been avoided, but the Soviets still had missile sites in Cuba and the USA still wanted them removed. The answer appeared to come on 26 October, when Khrushchev sent Kennedy a telegram offering to remove missiles from Cuba if the Americans agreed not to invade.

Before Kennedy could respond, another telegram arrived on 27 October, saying Khrushchev would remove the missiles only if US missiles in Turkey were also removed. On the same day an American U-2 plane was shot down over Cuba. The Hawks* in the USA demanded military action, but Kennedy refused to take that route.

Instead, he decided to ignore the second telegram and agreed to Khrushchev's proposal to pledge not to invade Cuba, in return for dismantling the missile sites. On 28 October, Khrushchev sent his agreement.

We now know that Kennedy's brother, Robert had met the Soviet ambassador in Washington the day before and agreed to remove the Turkish missiles. However, this part of the deal was kept secret.

The consequences of the Cuban Missile Crisis

The Cuban Missile Crisis made clear what could happen if the Soviet Union or the USA continued to follow a policy of brinkmanship*. Both Khrushchev and Kennedy had come under pressure to take action that could have led to full-scale war. Fortunately, this had not happened and both countries now wanted to make sure that future misunderstandings would not cause war to break out. Four important steps were taken:

- In June 1963, a direct communications line was set up between Washington and Moscow. This became known as the 'hotline'.

- In August 1963, a Test Ban Treaty was signed by the United States, Soviet Union and Great Britain. The three states agreed to prohibit the testing of nuclear weapons in outer Space, underwater or in the atmosphere. This was an important step towards the control of nuclear weapons.

- In 1967, the Outer Space Treaty was signed. As the USA and Soviet Union began a 'Space race', competing to explore Earth's orbit, the Moon and beyond, the possibility of launching a military attack from Space was starting to look realistic. In this treaty, the USA and Soviet Union agreed not to use Space for military purposes. The treaty specifically ruled out putting nuclear weapons into orbit.

- In 1968, the Nuclear Non-Proliferation* Treaty was signed to stop the spread of nuclear weapons. Countries that signed up to the treaty agreed not to share their nuclear technology with other countries.

Key terms

Brinkmanship*

Pushing disagreements to the point where there is a risk of war. In 1956 a former US Secretary of State, John Foster Dulles, wrote, 'If you are scared to go to the brink, you are lost'.

Non-proliferation*

Stopping the spread of something, usually weapons or armaments.

Extend your knowledge

Nuclear non-proliferation treaties – who signed?

The USA and Soviet Union were the most important countries to sign the treaties limiting the spread of nuclear weapons but they were not the only ones. The UK and France also had nuclear weapons and signed up, as did many countries around the world that did not have nuclear weapons. Some countries including Israel, Pakistan and India, either never signed the treaty or developed nuclear weapons regardless.

In some ways the Cuban Missile Crisis actually led to the world becoming a safer place. It also led to a change in relations between Kennedy and Khrushchev. Kennedy had shown himself to be a strong leader, not only in standing up to Khrushchev, but also in confronting the Hawks in his own government. His popularity increased significantly in the United States, particularly as the agreement over Turkey had not been made public. This increased popularity gave him more confidence in his dealings with the Soviet Union.

Khrushchev claimed that he had been the victor in the dispute, as he had guaranteed the security of Cuba (see Source F). However, this was not the feeling in Moscow, where the military felt that they had been forced into a humiliating withdrawal. The unpopularity was a significant factor in Khrushchev's dismissal in 1964.

Source F

An extract from Khrushchev's memoirs, published in 1967.

We sent the Americans a note saying that we agreed to remove our missiles and bombers on condition that President Kennedy gave us assurances that there would be no invasion of Cuba. Finally Kennedy gave in and agreed to make a statement giving us such an assurance. It was a great victory for us – a spectacular success without having to fire a single shot.

Source G

A cartoon published in the Washington Post on 1 November 1962.

A 1962 Herblock Cartoon, © The Herb Block Foundation

Extend your knowledge

Deadly nuclear power

Researchers at Harvard University worked out that if the USA and Soviet Union had fired nuclear missiles at each other during the Cuba crisis, then 100 million people would have been killed in the United States and another 100 million in the Soviet Union. That would have meant the death of 53.6% of the population in the United States and 44.6% in the Soviet Union.

Activities

1 'The Cuban Missile Crisis was won by President Kennedy'. With a partner, discuss whether you agree with this statement.

2 Read Source F – does this source make you surprised that Khrushchev was sacked in 1964?

3 Look at Source G. In your own words describe the cartoonist's view of the Cuban Missile Crisis. Do you agree?

Exam-style question

Explain the importance of the 'Bay of Pigs' invasion for relations between the USA and the Soviet Union   **8 marks**

Exam tip

Note the question asks about importance and also gives you a context for that importance – relations between the USA and the Soviet Union. Don't just say what happened. Explain how the invasion affected relations. Did it make them better or worse?

Summary

- The pro-American government in Cuba was overthrown.
- The USA supported Cuban exiles trying to restore a pro-American government.
- Castro turned to the Soviet Union for support.
- Khrushchev decided to site nuclear missiles in Cuba.
- Kennedy set up a naval blockade resulting in a tense stand-off known as the 'Thirteen Days'.

Checkpoint

Strengthen

S1 What actions did Castro take which worried the USA?

S2 Briefly summarise the events of the 'Thirteen Days'.

S3 What positive things happened as a result of the Cuban Missile Crisis?

Challenge

C1 If you were Kennedy, how would you counter the argument that supporting the 'Bay of Pigs' invasion was foolish?

C2 Why didn't the USA attack the Soviet ships, bringing missiles to Cuba?

C3 Why do you think the Cuban Missile Crisis is remembered as such as important event?

How confident do you feel about your answers to these questions? Re-read the section and then try answering the questions again. If you're still not sure, discuss with your teacher.

Learning outcomes

- Understand why Dubcek introduced reform in Czechoslovakia.
- Know about the Soviet reaction to the reforms.
- Understand the impact of the 'Prague Spring' on international relations.

Timeline

The 'Prague Spring' and its impact, 1968–69

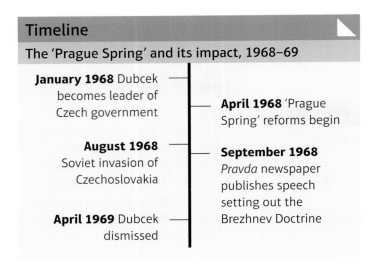

January 1968 Dubcek becomes leader of Czech government

April 1968 'Prague Spring' reforms begin

August 1968 Soviet invasion of Czechoslovakia

September 1968 *Pravda* newspaper publishes speech setting out the Brezhnev Doctrine

April 1969 Dubcek dismissed

Opposition to Soviet control

In 1948, Stalin had supported a coup in Czechoslovakia which removed non-communists from power and established a pro-Soviet communist government under the leadership of the head of the Czech communist party, Klement Gottwald (see pages 17–18).

Life under communist rule was difficult for the Czech people. In effect, the country was ruled by the Soviet Union, which used the secret police to maintain control. The Czech economy was run for the benefit of the Soviet Union and there were few consumer goods for the Czech people. There was no freedom of speech and radio, newspapers and television were censored. On Stalin's orders, the Czech government carried out purges between 1949 and 1954 and the victims included not only democratic politicians, but also military leaders, Catholics, Jews, people with wartime connections with the West and even high-ranking communists. Protests against the low standard of living and lack of freedom grew, with student demonstrations in 1966 showing how unpopular the government was.

The 'Prague Spring'

In 1968, Alexander Dubcek was elected as First Secretary of the Czech Communist Party – in effect, the head of the Czech government. The Soviet leadership approved of Dubcek and trusted him to make the government of Czechoslovakia more effective and less unpopular, while keeping the country completely loyal to the Soviet Union.

Dubcek was committed to the Warsaw Pact and a devoted communist. He believed that communism was the right political path but should not make life miserable. A communist government should offer 'socialism* with a human face'. He thought citizens should be able to enjoy life, express their views in public and speak out against Communist Party decisions they did not like, without fear of being punished by the government.

Key term

Socialism*

Communist countries sometimes refer to themselves as 'socialist'. For example, the Soviet Union was also known as the Union of Soviet Socialist Republics.

The reforms Dubcek introduced from April became known as the 'Prague Spring', after the country's capital.

- Censorship was relaxed and criticism of government actions was allowed.
- Trade unions were given wider powers and government control of industry was reduced.
- More power was given to the Czech regional governments.
- Trade with the West was increased.
- Czech people were given greater freedom to travel abroad.

- The idea of having multi-party elections was discussed, though Dubcek and other Communist leaders emphasised that this would not happen for many years.

Dubcek's reforms were met with great enthusiasm by the Czech people, but they were much less popular in Moscow. Dubcek was careful to assure Moscow that Czechoslovakia would remain in the Warsaw Pact and was a loyal ally of the Soviet Union.

However, the Soviet leader, Brezhnev (who replaced Khrushchev in 1968), disapproved of many of the measures Dubcek was proposing. If these measures were introduced in Czechoslovakia, wouldn't the other Warsaw Pact countries want similar reforms? At this time, Romania was refusing to attend Warsaw Pact meetings and the Yugoslavian leader, Tito, refused to accept control from Moscow. What if Moscow also lost control of Czechoslovakia?

Extend your knowledge

Yugoslavia

At the end of the Second World War, Yugoslavia was liberated largely without Soviet help. Although its leader, Josip Broz Tito was a communist, he did not want to follow Moscow's leadership and in 1948, Yugoslavia was expelled from Cominform. Tito was famous for once writing an open letter to Stalin telling him to stop sending people to kill Tito, or Tito would have to send someone to kill Stalin.

Figure 2.4 The Warsaw Pact troops that helped put down the 'Prague Spring' came from East Germany, Hungary and the Soviet Union.

The Soviet reaction

Throughout the months after Dubcek became leader, Brezhnev remained in contact, urging him not to endanger communism in Czechoslovakia by going too far with his reforms. He also ordered Warsaw Pact troops to carry out manoeuvres in Czechoslovakia to threaten Dubcek. When Dubcek invited Ceausescu of Romania and Tito of Yugoslavia to Prague for talks, Brezhnev decided to take action.

On 20 August 1968, 500,000 Warsaw Pact troops invaded Czechoslovakia and ended the 'Prague Spring'. There was little opposition to the invasion. Brezhnev had ordered the Czech army to remain in its barracks, just in case it tried to fight back. The Czech people could do little against such a powerful force, though there were individual acts of bravery, such as blocking roads or attacking individual tanks. The invading forces were told that they had been invited to help restore law and order by the Czech government. They were shocked by the hostility they encountered.

Source A

Czech citizens inspect a captured Soviet tank in Prague in August 1968.

Source B

A young journalist describes the moment when the Soviet troops arrived.

```
I remember very well the face of the first
Soviet soldier I saw. He was carrying a huge
machine gun, and looked like he'd just stepped
out of a film about the battle of Stalingrad.
He was very dirty, and his face was full of
sweat. It was absolutely ridiculous, absolutely
absurd. I tried to talk to him, but it was
pointless, he wouldn't speak to me. Even later
on, when I did manage to speak to some of the
soldiers, it was useless. They were totally
indoctrinated. They believed they had prevented
the outbreak of World War III or something.
```

Extend your knowledge

Jan Palach

Palach was a 20-year-old university student when, on 16 January 1969, he set himself on fire in Wenceslas Square in Prague as a protest against the Soviet occupation of his country. He died three days later.

Dubcek was arrested, sent to Moscow and ordered to reverse his reforms. Then in 1969 he was dismissed from office and replaced by Gustav Husak. Husak was a hardliner loyal to Moscow and introduced a clampdown in which over a thousand Czechs were arrested. For the next 20 years the country was firmly under Soviet-approved communist rule.

Activities

1. In a small group, list as many reasons as you can for why communism was unpopular in Czechoslovakia before 1968.

2. Look at the list of measures Dubcek proposed in the 'Prague Spring'. Explain how each one might make communism more popular.

3. Can you think of any reason why Brezhnev sent Dubcek back to Prague in 1968, instead of dismissing him straight away?

The Brezhnev Doctrine

To many in the West, Brezhnev's actions looked like an aggressive attempt to dominate another European country. However, the Soviet Union justified the invasion as a necessity to protect the unity of the communist movement in Europe. On 26 September 1968, the Soviet paper, *Pravda*, set out what was to become known as the Brezhnev Doctrine*. Brezhnev said that the actions of any individual communist country affected all communist countries. So if one country's actions threaten other countries, then it was the duty of those countries to take steps to stop those actions. What he was really saying was that all communist countries would be prevented from introducing reforms to make their country more liberal.

Key term

Doctrine*
A belief or philosophy.

Source C

The Brezhnev Doctrine, as explained in the Soviet newspaper *Pravda* in September 1968.

```
Every communist party is responsible not only
to its own people, but also to... the entire
communist movement. Whoever forgets this is
placing sole emphasis on the independence of
their own communist party and shirking their
international obligations.
```

The impact of the 'Prague Spring' and the Soviet invasion

The impact in Czechoslovakia...	The invasion ended the 'Prague Spring'. The authorities soon put things back to 'normal'.
The impact on relations between other communist countries in Europe...	Yugoslavia and Romania condemned the Soviet invasion, straining relations between their governments and Moscow. The Communist Parties of Italy and France cut links to Moscow. The governments of East Germany and Poland welcomed Brezhnev's actions. They could feel more secure that they would not be challenged by reformers in their own countries. The suppression of the 'Prague Spring' led to greater Soviet control of the members of the Warsaw Pact. This was reinforced by the Brezhnev Doctrine which emphasised that members of the Warsaw Pact were under the close control of the Soviet Union.
The impact on relations between the USA and the Soviet Union...	The USA and other Western governments were outraged by the invasion and many of them made strong protests to the Soviet Union. There was an attempt to pass a formal resolution condemning the invasion in the United Nations but this was vetoed by the Soviet Union. The Soviet Union saw that while the USA might make protests, it would not take direct action to oppose the Soviet Union in Europe.
The impact on the USA's international reputation...	At this time, the USA was involved in a costly war in North Vietnam and was also beginning to adopt a policy of détente with the Soviet Union. Other countries saw that the USA was keen to criticise the Soviet Union but much less prepared to take action.

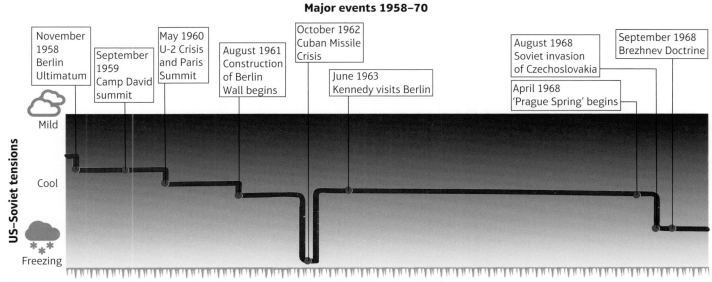

Figure 2.5 Rising and falling tensions between the USA and Soviet Union, 1958–70.

Exam-style question

Explain **two** consequences of the election of Alexander Dubcek as First Secretary of the Czech Communist Party in January 1968.　　**8 marks**

Exam tip

This question asks about 'consequences' so think about what difference the election of Dubcek made. How did his election change things?

Summary

- Communist rule in Czechoslovakia became more unpopular.
- Dubcek introduced reforms in the 'Prague Spring'.
- Brezhnev warned Dubcek not to go too far with his reforms.
- When Dubcek did not halt his reforms, Brezhnev ordered tanks into Czechoslovakia.
- The Brezhnev Doctrine was issued.

Checkpoint

Strengthen

S1 How did Dubcek's reforms change Czechoslovakia?

S2 Why did Brezhnev disapprove of the reforms?

S3 Why do you think the period of reforms is known as the 'Prague Spring'?

Challenge

C1 Can you think of any reasons why Dubcek did not reverse his reforms when he found out Brezhnev did not approve?

C2 Why did Brezhnev make a public declaration (the Brezhnev Doctrine) instead of just telling each satellite country what he wanted?

C3 Do you think the events of the 'Prague Spring' increased or decreased support for communism in Europe?

How confident do you feel about your answers to these questions? Discuss any you are unsure about with a partner then try rewriting your answers together.

Recap: Cold War crises, 1958–70

Recall quiz

1. Why was Berlin divided?
2. Why was the Soviet Union worried about Berlin in the years 1958–61?
3. Who were the presidents of the USA from 1958 to 1970?
4. Who were the leaders of the Soviet Union from 1958 to 1970?
5. Why did Kennedy visit Berlin in 1963?
6. When did Fidel Castro gain power in Cuba?
7. What was the 'Bay of Pigs' incident?
8. What agreements were made as a result of the Cuban crisis?
9. What was the 'Prague Spring'?
10. How did Brezhnev react to the 'Prague Spring'?

Activities ?

1. Write a short paragraph explaining why events in Berlin in 1958 almost led to war.
2. Write a paragraph to explain why events in Cuba in 1962 almost led to war.
3. Write a short paragraph explaining why even 'socialism with a human face' in Czechoslovakia was not acceptable to the Soviet Union.

Exam-style question, Section A

Explain **two** of the following:

- the importance of Kennedy's 1963 speech for the future of Germany
- the importance of the 'Bay of Pigs' incident for the future of Cuba
- the importance of the 'Prague Spring' for relations between the USA and the Soviet Union.

16 marks

Exam tip

Remember that this question is not asking for a description of an event or policy. It is asking about why that event or policy was important. What difference did it make? Remember to pay attention to the **context**. The 'Prague Spring' might have been important in how it affected life inside Czechoslovakia but that's not what the third bullet point is asking about!

Writing historically: linking information

When you explain events and their consequences, you need to show how your ideas link together.

Learning outcomes

By the end of this lesson, you will understand how to:

- link ideas clearly and concisely, using present participles and non-finite clauses.

Definitions

Non-finite clause: a clause beginning with a non-finite verb. These can be:

- **a present participle:** a verb form ending in *-ing*, e.g. 'running', 'building', 'forming', 'falling', etc.
- **a past participle:** a verb form often ending in *-ed*, e.g. 'formed', 'happened', etc, although there are several exceptions, e.g. 'ran', 'built', 'fell', etc.
- **an infinitive:** the 'root' verb form, which often begins with 'to', e.g. 'to run', 'to build', 'to form'.

How can I link ideas using present participles?

You can structure sentences to link related ideas in a number of different ways. One way is to use a **present participle** to create a **non-finite clause**.

For example, look at all the different ways in which two sentences in the example answer below can be linked to this exam-style question:

Explain **two** consequences of the election of Alexander Dubcek as First Secretary of the Czech Communist Party in 1968. **(8 marks)**

| Dubcek reformed communism. | **+** | He introduced the idea of 'socialism with a human face'. | **=** |

Dubcek wanted to reform communism, introducing the idea of 'socialism with a human face'.

This present participle clearly and succinctly links the two points together.

1. Look at the sentences below. How could you link them using a present participle?

| Communist rule in Czechoslovakia became more unpopular. | **+** | This led to mass protests on the streets of Prague. | **=?** |
| Brezhnev was determined to re-establish Soviet control over Czechoslovakia. | **+** | He therefore ordered Warsaw Pact troops to march on Prague. | **=?** |

2. a. Choose **either** of the sentences above. How else could you link them? Experiment with two or three different ways.

   b. Which of your experiments expresses the information most clearly? Write a sentence explaining your choice.

How can I link ideas using other kinds of non-finite verbs?

There are three forms of non-finite verb:

- **Infinitives** (e.g. 'to open', 'to make', 'to mean')
- **Past participles** (e.g. 'opened', 'made', 'meant')
- **Present participles** (e.g. 'opening', 'making', 'meaning')

Compare the sentences below:

> *Dubcek was determined to give socialism a 'human face'. He introduced political and social reforms.*

This non-finite clause allows the writer to connect these two points much more neatly.

> *Determined to give socialism a 'human face', Dubcek introduced political and social reforms.*

Now compare these sentences:

> *Brezhnev ordered Warsaw Pact troops to invade Czechoslovakia. He wanted them to restore Soviet control.*

This non-finite verb allows the writer to connect these two points much more neatly.

> *Brezhnev ordered Warsaw Pact troops to invade Czechoslovakia, to restore Soviet control.*

3. Write as many sentences as you can linking these points using non-finite verbs.

> *Dubcek introduced social and political reforms.*
>
> *Brezhnev ordered him not to go too far with his reforms.*
>
> *Dubcek did not listen to Brezhnev.*
>
> *Brezhnev ordered Warsaw Pact troops to march on Prague.*

Did you notice?

Non-finite clauses can often be positioned at different points in a sentence without affecting its meaning. Experiment with one or two of the sentences above, trying the non-finite clause in different positions.

Improving an answer

4. Look at the points noted below in response to this exam-style question:

> Explain the importance of the 'Bay of Pigs' invasion for relations between the USA and Soviet Union. **(8 marks)**

The US government had criticised the Soviet Union for interfering in other countries' affairs.

> *The US government was publicly exposed as interfering in other countries' affairs.*
>
> *The Cuban people supported their pro-communist government against the invaders.*
>
> *Fidel Castro asked the Soviet Union for support.*
>
> *Khrushchev decided to place Soviet missiles on Cuba.*

a. Experiment with different ways of linking some or all of the points using non-finite verbs.

b. Look carefully at all of the sentences you have written. Which ones work well, clearly and briefly linking ideas? Which do not? Use your findings to write a final re-draft of the notes above, aiming to make your sentences as clear and concise as possible.

03 | The end of the Cold War, 1970–91

The events in Berlin, Cuba and Czechoslovakia in the 1960s had highlighted just how far apart thinking was in Moscow and Washington. But one area where there was agreement was that the nuclear arms race threatened the future of mankind. This is one reason why the 1970s saw an attempt to improve relations through a policy known as détente. By the end of that decade, however, relations had once more deteriorated to a point where there was a 'Second Cold War' as President Ronald Reagan took a much tougher approach towards the Soviet Union.

When Mikhail Gorbachev became Soviet leader in 1985, he realised that his country could no longer afford the cost of the nuclear arms race and that radical changes were needed to how the Soviet Union was governed. Little did he realise that his policies would bring about, not only an end to the Cold War, but also the break-up of the Soviet Union.

Learning outcomes

When you have finished studying this chapter you will:

- know about the ways the USA and Soviet Union worked together to reduce the threat of nuclear war in the 1970s

- understand how relations deteriorated into a 'Second Cold War'

- understand how Soviet control of Eastern Europe came to an end.

3.1 Attempts to reduce tension between East and West, 1969–79

Timeline

Détente, 1969–79

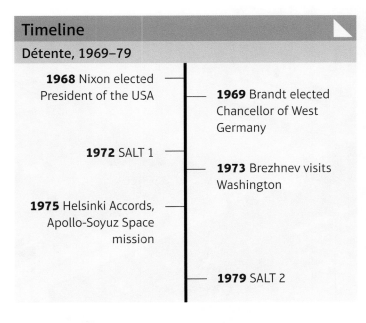

1968 Nixon elected President of the USA

1969 Brandt elected Chancellor of West Germany

1972 SALT 1

1973 Brezhnev visits Washington

1975 Helsinki Accords, Apollo-Soyuz Space mission

1979 SALT 2

Détente

After the Second World War, an arms race developed between the USA and the Soviet Union. Part of this arms race involved developing missiles which could carry nuclear warheads into enemy territory. Each country's scientists worked to develop weapons that would give their side an advantage. Soon, both the Soviet Union and America had enough long-distance weapons to completely destroy their rivals. With this great firepower, the result of war would be 'Mutually Assured Destruction' (MAD). So neither country's leaders wanted to risk a war which would lead to their own destruction.

However, the Cuban Missile Crisis (see page 49) showed that even if the leaders of the USA and Soviet Union didn't want to war they could lose control of events: a devastating war could break out almost by accident. During the 1970s, there was a genuine attempt to have a more co-operative and stable relationship. The policy has generally been referred to as détente*.

Extend your knowledge

The ongoing arms race

In 1957, the USA developed inter-continental ballistic missiles (ICBM). Within a year, the Soviet Union had them too. In 1960, the Americans developed submarine-launched ballistic missiles (SLBM). The Soviets had these from 1968. In the same year, they developed anti-ballistic missiles (ABM), designed to intercept ICBMs. The Americans developed their own four years later.

Why did the USA and the Soviet Union follow a policy of détente at this time?

Apart from the understandable desire to avoid plunging the world into nuclear war, both the USA and the Soviet Union had internal reasons for improving relations in the late 1960s and early 1970s.

In 1968, Richard Nixon was elected president of the USA. He was determined to take his country out of the Vietnam War, which had cost the USA billions of dollars and resulted in the deaths of almost 60,000 American soldiers.

There had also been large-scale demonstrations against the war in the USA (which sometimes ended in violence) and many Americans thought the USA should take a less active role in international affairs. The USA also had many social problems. Inequality between rich and poor, white and black, led to urban rioting on a massive scale in 1968, triggered by the assassination of the civil rights leader Martin Luther King.

Key term

Détente*

A period of peace between two groups that were previously at war, or hostile to each other.

A policy of détente with the Soviet Union would allow the USA to spend less money on weapons and more on trying to solve the social problems that had led to the riots of 1968.

Source A

The aftermath of rioting on the streets of Chicago, in April 1968, after the assassination of Martin Luther King.

The Soviet Union was facing economic problems and wanted to cut spending on weapons and devote more resources to improving living standards and updating its economy.

The Soviets also felt this was a relatively good time to look for better relations with the USA. They felt they were the USA's equals in nuclear weapons capability and the Vietnam War had shown that the USA military was not unbeatable. Improving relations and spending less on weapons would be a 'safe' policy.

- Wants to focus on ending the Vietnam War
- Needs to address social problems that led to large-scale rioting in 1968
- Building nuclear weapons is expensive.

DÉTENTE

Both countries:
- Can spend less money on nuclear weapons
- Have more money and time to concentrate on other issues.

- Poor living standards
- Economy is not developing
- Building nuclear weapons is expensive.

Figure 3.1 A summary of reasons why the USA and Soviet Union pursued a policy of détente in the 1970s.

There was also pressure for improved relations coming from Europe. In 1969, Willy Brandt was elected Chancellor of West Germany. He followed a policy of 'Ostpolitik', which involved building better relations between East and West Germany. Other European nations followed his lead and began establishing better relations with East European countries.

Extend your knowledge

Henry Kissinger and détente

One of the key figures in America's policy of détente was Henry Kissinger, who won the Nobel Peace Prize for his part in negotiating an end to US involvement in Vietnam. In 1969, the US president, Richard Nixon, appointed Kissinger as national security adviser and in 1973 he took Kissinger with him on a visit to the Soviet Union.

SALT 1

Perhaps the most important agreement between the USA and Soviet Union during the period of détente was the Strategic Arms Limitation Treaty (SALT 1) signed in May 1972. The treaty was the result of several years of difficult negotiations between the USA and the Soviet Union about which weapons should be limited. The treaty set out agreements in three areas:

- The Anti-Ballistic Missile Treaty stated that ABMs were allowed at only two sites. Each site should have a maximum of 100 missiles.

- The Interim* Treaty placed restrictions on the number of ICBMs and SLBMS each country could have. The USA was allowed 1,054 ICBMs and 740 SLBMs. The Soviet Union was allowed 1,618 ICBMs and 740 SLBMs. The Soviet Union was allowed more ICBMs because the USA already had more strategic bombers.

- The Basic Principles Agreement laid down rules for the conduct of nuclear warfare (such as banning the placing of warheads on the seabed) and set out steps for avoiding a nuclear war. For example, both countries agreed to exercise restraint in their relations and if war looked likely, 'to make every effort to avoid this risk'.

Key term

Interim*

Temporary, short-term. The treaty was called 'Interim' because the restrictions only applied until 1977.

SALT 1 had a number of weaknesses. In reality, if nuclear war looked likely, it was unrealistic to expect it could be avoided just because the countries had signed a piece of paper, especially as both countries still owned more than enough nuclear weapons to destroy the other many times over. It was also true that the treaty did not cover the latest technological development, multiple independently targeted re-entry vehicles (MIRVs), which carried multiple nuclear warheads on a single missile.

However, SALT 1 did have a significant impact on international relations. Whatever its faults, it had major symbolic importance. Both the USA and the Soviet Union wanted to reach agreement and wanted to demonstrate their better relations publicly.

Shortly after signing SALT 1, Nixon visited Brezhnev in Moscow, and in 1973 the Soviet leader came to Washington. In 1974 negotiations began for SALT 2, in which it was hoped agreement would be found on matters not resolved in SALT 1.

Activities ?

1 Write a paragraph explaining why the USA and the Soviet Union decided to follow a policy of détente in the 1970s.

2 Pick one of the following statements and prepare a short talk (no more than 30 seconds) in support of the statement:

   a SALT 1 was a valuable move towards world peace.

   b SALT 1 had too many weaknesses to be considered a valuable agreement.

Source B

President Nixon with the Soviet leader, Brezhnev during their meeting at the White House in 1973.

The Helsinki Accords, 1975

In 1973, 33 nations from NATO and the Warsaw Pact met to build on the spirit of co-operation which had been established in SALT 1. In August 1975, an announcement was made to say agreement had been reached in three areas, which the conference organisers described as 'baskets':

Borders are inviolable, they cannot be altered by force.

1. EUROPEAN BORDERS

We will continue to work for closer relations between Western and Soviet-controlled countries. This will include trade agreements, technology exchanges and a joint Space mission.

2. INTERNATIONAL CO-OPERATION

We will respect human rights and individual freedoms such as free speech, religion, and free movement across Europe.

3. HUMAN RIGHTS

Figure 3.2 The main agreements covered in the three 'baskets' of the Helsinki Accords.

Source C

The Soviet–American team of astronauts and cosmonauts that worked on the Apollo-Soyuz mission of 1975.

Basket 1 was very significant as this was the first time that the boundaries between East and West Germany and the existing boundaries of the Soviet-controlled countries were formally accepted.

The spirit of co-operation described in **Basket 2** was followed up that same year with a joint USA–Soviet Space mission.

The Helsinki Accord was the high point of détente. It seemed to mark the dawn of a new approach to international relations. But even in drawing up the agreements, the USA and the Soviet Union were still, to some extent, playing Cold War politics.

What Brezhnev wanted from the agreements was recognition of existing borders and an opportunity to boost the Soviet economy. So while he was very pleased with Baskets 1 and 2, some American politicians were very unhappy with them (see Source D).

What the USA wanted was an extension of human rights into Soviet-controlled territories, which would undermine communist authority and weaken the power of the Soviet Union. So, while the Americans were pleased with **Basket 3**, the Soviets were concerned that organisations would be set up to monitor Soviet policies in its satellite states (see Source E).

Source D

The Helsinki Accords were signed by President Gerald Ford on behalf of the USA.

History will judge this conference not by what we say here today, but by what we do tomorrow. Not by the promises we make, but by the promises we keep.

Mr. Ford flew halfway round the world to sign an agreement at Helsinki which placed the American seal of approval on the Soviet Empire in Eastern Europe.

Source E

Comments made by the Soviet Ambassador to the United Nations about the Helsinki Accords.

The members of the Politburo read the full text. They had no objections when they read the first and second sections. When they got to the third 'humanitarian' section, their hair stood on end. Some said it was a complete betrayal of communist ideology. But Gromyko came up with this argument. The main thing about the Helsinki treaty is the recognition of the borders. That is what we shed our blood for in the Great Patriotic War. All 35 signatories are now saying these are the borders of Europe. As for human rights, Gromyko said, 'Well, who's the master of this house? We are the master and it will be up to us how we decide to act. Who can force us?'

SALT 2

Talks working towards a second SALT continued until 18 June 1979, when President Carter for the USA and President Brezhnev for the Soviet Union signed a highly complex and technical agreement. It included restrictions on missile launchers and strategic bombers, as well as a ban on testing or deploying new types of ICBM.

However, the improved relations between the Soviet Union and USA that had existed for much of the 1970s were beginning to fade.

- In the USA, there was a growing belief amongst both Democrats (President Carter's party) and Republicans that the Soviet government could not be trusted. There had been an increase in Soviet support for communist groups in countries such as El Salvador, Nicaragua and Angola. Any agreement with the Soviet Union was seen by some Americans as a sign of weakness.
- In November 1979, Islamic militants captured the American embassy in Tehran (capital of Iran). American diplomats and their families were publically humiliated and more than 60 of them held hostage for 444 days. Many angry Americans wanted to see an end to détente and for America to restore its position as a powerful nation that took strong measures against anyone threatening its interests.
- Even within President Carter's own administration, advisers such as Zbigniew Brzezinski called for a stronger stance to be taken against the Soviet Union.
- Finally, in December 1979, the Soviet Union invaded Afghanistan, bringing the period of détente to an end.

When the Soviet Union entered Afghanistan, SALT 2 was still going through the process of ratification* by the American government. President Carter felt he could no longer support the treaty and it was withdrawn from the Senate.

Key term

Ratification*

Formal approval. If the Senate had ratified SALT 2, the terms would have become official US policy.

Activities ?

1. Agreement was made on three 'baskets' at Helsinki. Which one do you think was the most important for relations between the USA and the Soviet Union? Explain your answer.

2. Some historians thought that the seizure of American hostages in Iran helped bring an end to détente. Can you explain the link between the two events?

Exam-style question, Section A

Write a narrative account analysing the key events of détente in the years 1970–79.

You may use the following in your answer:

- SALT 1, 1972
- The Helsinki Accords, 1975.

You **must** also use information of your own. **8 marks**

Exam tip

Remember that the key to scoring well on this type of question is to create a coherent narrative that links together events and explains how one leads to the next in a logical and structured way.

Summary

- The events of the 1960s had worried world leaders about the threat of nuclear war.
- The arms race increased that worry.
- Both the USA and the Soviet Union had domestic reasons for wanting to improve relations.
- There was a series of agreements to limit nuclear weapons in the 1970s.
- By the end of the 1970s, the spirit of co-operation had died.

Checkpoint

Strengthen

S1 What was 'MAD'?

S2 What were the weaknesses of SALT 1?

S3 Why was SALT 2 not ratified by the USA?

Challenge

C1 Why was 'MAD' not necessarily bad?

C2 How did the policy of 'Ostpolitik' influence events in the 1980s?

C3 What different aims did world leaders have in the Helsinki Accords.

How confident do you feel about your answers to these questions? Form a small group and discuss any questions you are not sure about. Look for the answers in this section. Now rewrite your answers as a group.

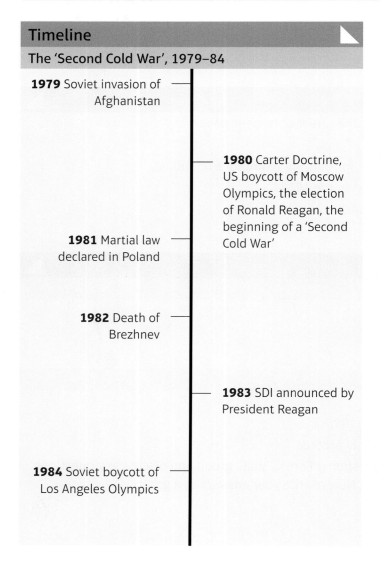

Timeline
The 'Second Cold War', 1979–84

1979 Soviet invasion of Afghanistan

1980 Carter Doctrine, US boycott of Moscow Olympics, the election of Ronald Reagan, the beginning of a 'Second Cold War'

1981 Martial law declared in Poland

1982 Death of Brezhnev

1983 SDI announced by President Reagan

1984 Soviet boycott of Los Angeles Olympics

The Soviet invasion of Afghanistan, 1979

Why was the Soviet Union interested in Afghanistan?

Afghanistan was viewed by the Soviet Union as an important neighbour. In 1979, a revolution in Iran deposed the Shah*. He was replaced by a Muslim fundamentalist government. Afghanistan now formed an important buffer between Iran and the Soviet Union. Moscow was determined not to let Muslim fundamentalism spread across its borders: the Soviet Union had many Muslim citizens. To protect Soviet interests, it was important to ensure that there was a pro-Soviet government in Afghanistan.

Key term

Shah*

King or emperor. Iran was ruled by shahs until the 1979 revolution.

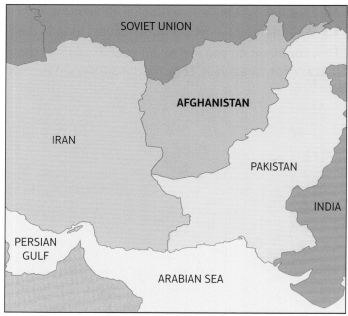

Figure 3.3 Afghanistan in 1979 and its borders with the Soviet Union, Pakistan and Iran.

Build-up to the invasion

In April 1978, a pro-Soviet government took control in Afghanistan and received economic assistance from Moscow. It was toppled in September 1979 when Hafizullah Amin staged a popular coup. At first, Moscow supported Amin, but his government became increasingly unpopular as other pro-Muslim factions tried to overthrow him. When Brezhnev heard rumours that Amin was talking to the USA about possible American support, he decided to act.

Event Itsely:

On 24 December 1979, Soviet forces invaded Afghanistan. They claimed that they had been invited in by Amin to support his government against terrorists. However, Amin was assassinated on 27 December (almost certainly by Soviet commandos) and replaced by the pro-Soviet Babrak Kamal. The Soviets remained in Afghanistan for almost ten years, fighting opponents of Babrak Kamal.

Source A

Afghan mujahideen standing on a captured Soviet tank, 18 January 1980.

The American reaction

The Soviet Union invaded Afghanistan to protect its interests in a neighbouring state. It saw the situation as very similar to that in Czechoslovakia (see Chapter 2). But the Americans believed this was an example of the Soviet Union attempting to spread communism abroad, which they had worked to resist.

President Carter went as far as to claim the invasion posed the biggest threat to world peace since the end of the Second World War. He withdrew the SALT 2 proposal (page 72) from the Senate and increased spending on arms. In his state of the union speech to the American people in January 1980, he said that the USA would repel by force, if necessary, any threat to American interests in the Persian Gulf. This became known as the Carter

Key term

Economic sanctions*

Measures taken to damage a country's economy, usually involving a trade ban.

Doctrine and was deliberately modelled on the Truman Doctrine (page 20) to show its importance. Carter also imposed economic sanctions* on the Soviet Union and began sending weapons and funds to the mujahideen.

The impact of the invasion on USA–Soviet relations

Détente was already close to breaking up before the Soviet invasion of Afghanistan. After the invasion it was finished. Some historians argue that the Americans deliberately over-reacted to the Soviet invasion because they were looking for a way to 'get out' of détente. If so, they had found their way.

In the 1980 presidential election in the USA, the Republican candidate, Ronald Reagan, ridiculed President Carter as weak and argued that the time had come for America to reclaim its position on the world stage and stand up to communism. He won a landslide victory.

Although US–Soviet relations were becoming more confrontational, the invasion of Afghanistan made confrontation more of a certainty. It helped bring about the election of a US president who believed communism was 'evil' and should be actively opposed.

THINKING HISTORICALLY ▷ **Cause and Consequence (2c)**

Far-reaching consequences

Most events have multiple consequences. Their impact can often be felt in many different 'strands' of history, e.g. the Wall Street Crash had economic consequences, but also affected society, politics and international relations. The Soviet Union's decision to invade Afghanistan was a significant event in the Cold War that had consequences in several different areas.

1   How many consequences have been identified? Do you think this list is complete? If no, what has been missed?

2   Suggest a category (e.g. international relations, government, social, economic) for each consequence. How many categories have you ended up with?

3   Which of these consequences do you think the Soviet Union might have intended when the invasion of Afghanistan was planned?

4   Which of the consequences might a historian writing a history of the Cold War **not** refer to? Explain your answer.

5   Write one historical question about the invasion of Afghanistan that might require the historian to know about all these consequences in order to answer it well.

The Olympic boycotts

In protest against the invasion of Afghanistan, the USA led a boycott of the 1980 Olympic Games, which was held in Moscow. Over 60 nations supported the US boycott.

This was a highly significant move as the Olympic Games are a global event, which the Soviet Union was hoping to use to promote communism to the huge television audience who would watch the Olympics around the world. The boycott reflected the influence that the USA had in international affairs. All countries looked forward to the Olympics, and telling their athletes not to go was not an easy thing to do. Some countries, including Britain, did not prevent athletes from going, but did encourage them not to take part. Others allowed athletes to take part as individuals, rather than officially representing their country. But American athletes were told that if they tried to travel to Moscow, their passports would be taken away.

The boycott was so effective that with many of the best athletes staying away, some events at the Moscow games were made to look second-rate. The Soviet Union was extremely angry that its chance to showcase communism to the world had been undermined and relations with the USA deteriorated even further.

This was a significant moment in the 'Second Cold War'. Relations were so poor that even four years later, when it was the USA's turn to hold the Olympics in Los Angeles, in 1984, the Soviet Union led a boycott of the games which was joined by 15 communist countries.

Activities ?

1   Why did the Soviet Union invade Afghanistan?
2   What were the consequences of that invasion for international relations?
3   You have been appointed by Ronald Reagan to run his campaign against President Carter. Your message is 'Carter has been soft on the Soviets'. What arguments would you use to support your message?

Ronald Reagan and the 'Second Cold War'

Reagan's policies

President Reagan's tougher approach towards the Soviet Union led to a period of tense and hostile relations that is often referred to as the 'Second Cold War'. In reality, the change had already begun under President Carter, but it became much more obvious under Reagan.

- Reagan's mind-set was made clear in a speech to a Christian group in 1983, in which he described the Soviet Union as an 'evil empire' and said that the USA represented the forces of 'good'.

- Reagan persuaded the US Congress to boost America's armed forces by increasing spending on arms. In 1982, 13% more was spent, with a further 8% in 1983 and 1984. New weapons such as Trident submarines and Stealth bombers were developed.

- He announced the 'Reagan Doctrine': the USA would not only support anti-communist governments, but also anti-communist groups trying to overthrow communist governments. In line with this doctrine, support was given to insurgent groups in Central American countries including El Salvador and Nicaragua. US forces also invaded the Caribbean island of Grenada and toppled the communist government there. Reagan described this as the first 'rollback' of communist influence since the Second World War.

The Strategic Defense Initiative

President Reagan knew that the Soviet economy was struggling. So by increasing spending and support for anti-communists, he knew he could create real difficulties for the Soviet Union. It would need to find extra funding to counter the USA.

In 1983, Reagan announced a new policy that would place Soviet spending under even more pressure. The Strategic Defense Initiative (SDI), or 'Star Wars' as it was popularly called, would place a series of satellites in orbit. These satellites would carry powerful lasers that could shoot down Soviet missiles and prevent them from harming the USA. This was, of course, against the terms of the 1967 Outer Space Treaty (see page 55). Reagan spoke of SDI as a reality and did not admit to the world that the new system was years from being ready.

In Moscow, the news of the development was a complete shock. The Soviet Union had devoted huge resources to catching up with American missile technology. Now their missiles would be redundant and a new system was needed.

SDI was a significant turning point both in the arms race and the Cold War. The Soviet Union's leaders knew that they would have to invest huge sums to develop an equivalent system to SDI. The USA had made major advances in computer technology and the Soviet Union would have to catch up before it could even begin to consider building its own SDI system. But the Soviet economy was not strong enough. This was one important factor behind the 'new thinking' of Mikhail Gorbachev when he became Soviet leader in 1985.

Source B

Ronald Reagan announcing SDI in a televised address to the nation on 23 March 1983.

Activities ?

1   Look at Source B. What does the image on the easel show?

2   Source B is a still from a television address to the nation. Suggest reasons why the image on the easel has been placed there.

3   What was the Soviet reaction to the announcement of SDI? Why did it have such a major impact on relations between the USA and Soviet Union?

Source C

An extract from Ronald Reagan's autobiography, published in 1990.

During the late seventies, I felt our country had begun to abdicate* its historical role as the spiritual leader of the Free World and its foremost defender of democracy... . Predictably, the Soviets had interpreted our hesitation as reluctance to act and had tried to exploit it in their agenda to achieve a communist-dominated world... . I deliberately set out to say some frank things about the Soviets to let them know there were some new fellows in Washington.

Key term

Abdicate*

To step down from office or power.

Exam-style question, Section A

Explain the importance of the Soviet invasion of Afghanistan for relations between the USA and the Soviet Union. **8 marks**

Exam tip

The question asks about importance and also gives you a context for that importance – relations between the USA and the Soviet Union. So you are not asked to say why the Soviet Union invaded or how difficult they found it to win. Explain how the invasion affected relations. Did it make them better or worse?

Summary

- The Soviet Union was concerned about nationalism in Afghanistan.
- The USA saw Soviet intervention in Afghanistan as spreading communism.
- Relations between the USA and the Soviet Union deteriorated.
- Ronald Reagan was elected with a 'get tough on the communists' policy.
- A 'Second Cold War' began.

Checkpoint

Strengthen

S1 Who were the mujahideen?

S2 What was the Carter Doctrine?

S3 Explain how 'SDI' was supposed to work.

Challenge

C1 Why might some people argue that the Soviet invasion of Afghanistan served American purposes?

C2 How did Reagan's attitude to the Soviet Union differ from that of his predecessors?

C3 How important was 'SDI' in changing relations between the USA and the Soviet Union?

How confident do you feel about your answers to these questions? Form a small group and discuss any questions you are not sure about. Look for the answers in this section. Now rewrite your answers as a group.

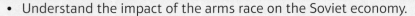
Timeline

End of the Cold War and Soviet Union, 1985–91

1985 Gorbachev becomes Soviet leader, Geneva Summit

1986 Reykjavik Summit

1987 Intermediate-Range Nuclear Force Treaty (INF)

1988 Moscow Summit

1989 Fall of Berlin Wall

1990 Gorbachev wins Nobel Prize

1991 Gorbachev overthrown, Soviet Union dissolves

Gorbachev's new thinking

Mikhail Gorbachev became leader of the Soviet Union in March 1985. At this time, the Soviet Union was facing a number of serious problems:

- During the Brezhnev era, huge sums were spent on developing arms to keep pace with the USA. Investment in the Soviet economy was low. There was barely any industrial growth in the Soviet Union or its satellite states in the mid-1980s. Standards of living in the East were nowhere near what could be found in the West.

- Low standards of living and the lack of human rights were leading to unrest in some satellite states. In Poland, the trade union 'Solidarity' posed such a threat to the communist government that it was banned. In 1981 the authorities declared martial law.

- Meanwhile, Soviet troops carried out manoeuvres along the Polish border, ready to invade, if necessary. In other Soviet satellite states, opposition to communist rule was only kept in check by the tight control of secret police forces, for example, the Stasi in East Germany and Securitate in Romania.

- The Soviet Union had suffered from poor leadership for many years.

- In recent years there had been a run of leaders in poor health, who ruled briefly and did not have time to make useful plans for the future. Brezhnev died in 1982 after a long illness. His successor Andropov died in 1984. Chernenko followed and died a year later.

Extend your knowledge

The Chernobyl disaster

In the early hours of 26 April 1986, there was an explosion in one of four nuclear reactors at the Chernobyl power station in the Soviet Union. The blast released more than one hundred times the radiation released by the Hiroshima atomic bomb. The Soviet authorities were reluctant to release full details of what happened, but we now know that over 350,000 people were moved out of the area to avoid radiation. Only 31 people died at the time, but it has been much more difficult to know how many people have died from cancers caused by radiation. The environmental group, Greenpeace, estimates that there will be 93,000 extra cancer deaths because of the explosion. However, despite the contamination, wildlife thrives in the exclusion zone.

Gorbachev knew that things had to change and is said to have told his wife in 1985, 'We can't go on living like this.' He was determined to reform communism in the Soviet Union and introduced a series of policies that would have a major impact on Soviet foreign policy and relations with the USA.

- Gorbachev proposed that the Soviet state and economy should be reformed to include some of the practices that made capitalism successful. This was called perestroika*.
- There should also be more openness and less corruption in government. People should not need to fear the state or fear expressing their opinions (see Source A). This policy of glasnost* would allow opposition to the government and give the people a better understanding of how the country was run.
- The Brezhnev Doctrine (see page 60), which had dominated the Soviet Union's relations with its satellite states and the West since the time of the 'Prague Spring', would now be dropped. The Soviet Union would no longer get involved in the domestic affairs of other communist countries.
- The Soviet Union would reduce spending on arms and defence and withdraw from Afghanistan.

The American response

At the same time as Gorbachev was adopting new policies in the Soviet Union, there was a change of thinking in the USA.

When Ronald Reagan had started his term as president in 1981, he promised that he would stand tough against communism. He had brought about a 'Second Cold War' with an increase in spending on arms and a more confrontational approach to the Soviet Union. However, when Gorbachev became Soviet leader in 1985, relations between the USA and the Soviet Union changed. Here was a Soviet leader who was not looking to expand communism, but instead, was determined to reform the Soviet Union from the inside, and moreover to work with the USA to reduce Cold War tensions.

Reagan saw that there was a real opportunity to end the Cold War and to adopt a more open approach to the Soviet Union, whilst at the same time sticking to his overall aim.

Gorbachev's new thinking in action

During the first four years of Gorbachev's leadership of the Soviet Union, significant steps were made to bring about further limitations on nuclear weapons.

Key terms

Perestroika*

Russian for 'reconstruction'. It was used in the Gorbachev era to describe his programme for reorganising and restructuring the Soviet state.

Glasnost*

Russian for 'openness' or 'transparency'. In the 1980s and 1990s, it was used to describe Gorbachev's new, more open, attitude to government and foreign relations.

Source A

A joke from the Soviet era.

A frightened man came to the KGB.

'My talking parrot has disappeared.'

'That's not the kind of case we handle. Go and make a report at the police station.'

'Excuse me, of course I know that I need to talk to the police. I've come here to make an official statement that I completely disagree with the parrot.'

Geneva Summit November 1985

Before the Geneva Summit, Gorbachev appointed a new foreign minister, Eduard Shevardnadze, to replace the old hardliner, Andrei Gromyko. At Geneva, Gorbachev and Reagan met for the first time.

Outcome

No formal agreements but Reagan and Gorbachev established a good working relationship, and a mutual desire to improve relations between their countries.

Reykjavik Summit October 1986

Gorbachev was worried about the danger that nuclear weapons posed to the world. His desire to reduce the world stockpile of nuclear arms may well have been strengthened when the Chernobyl nuclear power plant in Ukraine exploded in April 1986. Large swathes of the Soviet Union and beyond were affected by nuclear fallout. In Reykjavik, Gorbachev proposed phasing out nuclear weapons if the Americans gave up their SDI program.

Outcome

Both leaders knew that the Americans could not agree to give up SDI. Once again, the meeting broke up with no formal agreement but an improvement in relations.

Washington Summit December 1987

Gorbachev had now accepted that the Americans were not going to scrap SDI, and that his country's best interests lay in agreements on disarmament, reducing spending on weapons and better relations with the West.

Outcome

This was the first US–Soviet summit to lead to the signing of a formal treaty – the Intermediate-Range Nuclear Force (INF) Treaty. The treaty said that both countries would abolish all land-based missiles with a range of 500–5,500 km.

Moscow Summit 1988

In this summit, some complex detail related to the INF treaty was resolved. Later in the year, Gorbachev travelled to the USA, where he made a speech at the United Nations announcing a reduction in Warsaw Pact troops and that Soviet forces would leave Afghanistan.

Malta Summit 1989

At Malta, Gorbachev met with the new American president, George Bush.

Outcome

No new agreements were made, but both the USA and the Soviet Union saw this meeting as marking the end of the Cold War.

Gorbachev said, 'I assure the President of the United States that I will never start a hot war against the USA. We are at the beginning of a long road to a lasting, peaceful era. The threat of force, mistrust, psychological and ideological struggle should all be things of the past.' Bush said, 'We can realise a lasting peace and transform the East–West relationship to one of enduring co-operation.'

Figure 3.4 Landmark summit meetings between the US and Soviet leaders in the 1980s.

Source B

Reagan and Gorbachev sign the INF Treaty in Washington, in December 1987.

The end of the Soviet hold on Eastern Europe

Once Gorbachev had announced that the Soviet Union was giving up the Brezhnev Doctrine, the Soviet satellite countries were free to choose how they would be governed. They would no longer have to fear that the Soviets would intervene as they had in Hungary in 1956 (see page 32) and Czechoslovakia in 1968 (see page 58). Gorbachev's reforms within the Soviet Union, restructuring the economy and introducing more openness to government, further encouraged the people of the satellite states to introduce changes that would improve their standard of living and increase their individual freedoms.

Gorbachev's reforms were not intended to bring an end to communism. They were designed to introduce

June 1989: Poland
Solidarity is legalised and wins a landslide victory in Polish elections.

September 1989: East Germany
Huge numbers of East Germans leave for the West, travelling through Hungary to Austria. On 11 September, 125,000 East Germans cross the border.

October 1989: East Germany
Gorbachev refuses to help the East German government put down demonstrations.

November 1989: East Germany
The East German government announces that the border crossing to West Berlin will be opened. Thousands of East Berliners force their way through the crossing. People on both sides of the Berlin Wall start pulling it down. East and West Germany are formally reunited in 1990.

May 1989: Hungary
The government takes down the fence along the border with non-communist Austria. It promises a new democratic government, free elections are held in October.

November 1989: Czechoslovakia
The 'Velvet Revolution' overthrows the communist government. The anti-communist Vaclav Havel is elected president.

December 1989: Romania
There are demonstrations against the communist government. The communist leader, Ceausescu, is overthrown and executed.

December 1989: Bulgaria
The communist leader Peter Mladenov resigns live on national television. Free elections are held the following year.

December 1990: Yugoslavia
Slovenians vote to become independent in a free referendum. Yugoslavia breaks up as Croatia, Serbia and Montenegro, Bosnia-Herzegovina, Kosovo and Macedonia all declare independence during the 1990s.

Figure 3.5 The end of communist rule in Eastern Europe.

reforms that would strengthen communist government, both within the Soviet Union and within the satellite states in the Warsaw Pact. As it turned out, within twelve months of his speech at the United Nations, the communist system would be dismantled throughout Eastern Europe. A year after that, the Soviet Union itself was disbanded.

The significance of the fall of the Berlin Wall

On a personal level, for many citizens of East and West Germany, the fall of the Berlin Wall meant they could be reunited with relatives and friends who they had not seen for almost 30 years. There were scenes of great emotion as people realised that the restrictions that had prevented them from crossing the border were gone. People wanted to commemorate the day the Wall fell. For days after the border opened, they took hammers and chipped away to break off their own souvenir piece to take home.

In political terms, the fall of the Wall was mainly a symbolic event. By November 1989, East Germans could already travel to the West through Austria and the East German leader Erich Honecker had been sacked. Throughout Eastern Europe, communist governments

Source C

East Berliners climbing on the Wall on 11 November 1989.

Source D

A German, who was a 10-year-old living in East Germany when the Berlin Wall fell, describes visiting West Germany three months later.

> I went with my mother by train from Berlin. I remember the day very well; being excited and also a little nervous. We passed the border, and no one asked us for our passports or where we wanted to go — unimaginable only months earlier. We arrived and everything looked and felt different. Streets were clean, buildings and houses were kept well and the air did not smell of burnt brown coal. For a few days I felt like living in a different world. I returned home after a few days, and became aware of the large differences between East and West, in particular of the rundown, sad and dirty state that East Germany was in.

were falling and the Soviet Union showed it had no intention of stepping in to stop the wave of protest and demand for reform.

For 30 years the Berlin Wall had stood for the division of Europe. It was a symbol of the Cold War and of Soviet control. On 9 November 1989, its destruction became the symbol of the end of Soviet control and the end of the Cold War.

The end of the Warsaw Pact

The Warsaw Pact had been formed after the Western Allies set up NATO (see Chapter 1). Its creation formally established that Europe was divided into two armed camps and throughout the period of the Cold War the Warsaw Pact was seen as a potential threat to the democratic West. As far as the Soviet Union was concerned, of course, it was also a means to co-ordinate forces to defend the communist East from any threat from the West.

The Pact was also a symbol of Soviet dominance in Eastern Europe. It was a highly useful way for the Soviet Union to keep an eye on what its communist allies were doing and forcing decisions on them. So when Hungary and Czechoslovakia stepped out of line (in 1956 and 1968), it was Warsaw Pact forces that brought them back into the fold.

The events of 1989 saw communist governments coming under pressure across Eastern Europe and made it impossible for the Warsaw Pact to survive. Military co-operation between the member states ended in early 1990 and the Pact was formally dissolved in July 1991.

The end of the Pact was a highly significant moment in the history of the Cold War.

Europe was reunited

The formation of the Warsaw Pact had formally divided Europe in two. Now its break-up indicated that the division between democratic West and communist East was gone. The Cold War was over and there were no longer two armed alliances confronting each other across the 'Iron Curtain'. Indeed with the end of the Warsaw Pact and the Berlin Wall, the 'Iron Curtain' itself ceased to exist. The confrontational politics that had brought the world close to nuclear war on at least one occasion during the Cold War became a thing of the past.

Source E

Boris Yeltsin, president of the Russian republic, standing on top of a tank in August 1989. He is rallying support for Gorbachev. One of his supporters is waving a Russian flag.

The satellite states regained their independence

The end of the Pact led to many countries becoming truly independent of the Soviet Union and governing themselves for the first time in decades. They no longer had to follow policies created in Moscow, or run their economies to benefit the Soviet Union. After the Warsaw Pact was finished, every single one of its members abandoned communism.

Gorbachev fell from power

Losing control over the Soviet satellites played a major part in the downfall of Gorbachev in the Soviet Union. Hard-line communists blamed him for losing control over Eastern Europe and threatening Soviet security. His position became worse when the Baltic states of Lithuania, Latvia and Estonia all declared themselves independent of the Soviet Union during 1990.

In August 1991, the communist hardliners staged a coup against Gorbachev. Boris Yeltsin, the president of the Soviet republic of Russia rallied the people of Moscow to oppose the coup and Gorbachev continued in government, but the coup severely damaged his authority.

The leaders of the other Soviet republics took advantage of Gorbachev's weakness and 12 of them joined together in a Commonwealth of Independent States. Gorbachev could not continue under these circumstances and on 25 December 1991, he announced his resignation as Soviet leader. His resignation was immediately followed by the break-up of the Soviet Union.

Activity ?

In a small group, prepare a presentation explaining which of these two statements you agree with more. Include as much evidence as you can from this chapter.

a 'The Cold War came to an end because President Reagan's policies won it for the USA'.

b 'The Cold War came to an end because Mikhail Gorbachev was a weak leader'.

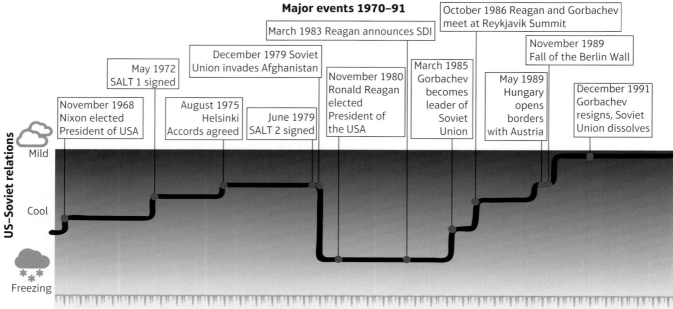

Figure 3.6 Relations between the USA and Soviet Union, 1968–91.

Exam-style question, Section A ⚪

Explain **two** consequences of Mikhail Gorbachev's decision to abandon the Brezhnev Doctrine. **8 marks**

Exam tip ⚪

This question asks about 'consequences' so we don't need a lot of information on **how** or **why** the Doctrine was abandoned. Instead concentrate your efforts on what **difference** abandoning it made. How did this change things?

Summary ◣

- The weakness of the Soviet economy led to a rethink of the country's role in international politics.
- Gorbachev's 'new thinking' encouraged a positive response from the USA.
- The Soviet Union abandoned the Brezhnev Doctrine.
- Nationalist uprisings resulted in the break-up of the Warsaw Pact.
- The Soviet Union was dissolved.

Checkpoint ◣

Strengthen

S1 When did Reagan and Gorbachev meet in Geneva?

S2 What was Gorbachev's 'new thinking'

S3 What were *perestroika* and *glasnost*?

Challenge

C1 What part did the Chernobyl disaster play in international relations in the 1980s?

C2 Why was the fall of the Berlin Wall so important?

C3 How significant was the end of the Warsaw Pact?

How confident do you feel about your answers to these questions? Re-read the chapter, making notes as you go. Now try answering the questions again.

Recall quiz

1 When were the Helsinki Accords signed?
2 What incident led to President Carter announcing the Carter Doctrine?
3 How did the Soviet Union retaliate when the USA boycotted the 1980 Olympics?
4 In which Warsaw Pact country was martial law declared in 1981?
5 What was SDI?
6 Name the Soviet leaders from 1982 to 1985.
7 What was the main agreement of the INF Treaty?
8 What happened on 9 November 1989?
9 Who helped Gorbachev stay in power when there was a coup in August 1991?
10 When did Gorbachev resign?

Activities ?

1 Write a short paragraph explaining why détente came to an end from 1979.
2 Why is the period 1979–85 sometimes called the 'Second Cold War'?
3 How important was Gorbachev's 'new thinking' in ending the Cold War?

Exam-style question, Section A

Explain **two** of the following:

- the importance of the nuclear arms race for relations between the USA and the Soviet Union
- the importance of the Soviet invasion of Afghanistan for relations between the USA and the Soviet Union
- the importance of Ronald Reagan for relations between the USA and the Soviet Union. **16 marks**

Exam tip

Remember that this question is not asking for a description of an event or policy. It is asking about why that event or policy was important. What **difference** did it make? Remember to pay attention to the context. All these developments are about relations between the USA and the Soviet Union.

Writing historically: narrative analysis

When you write a narrative analysis, you need to explain a series of events: their causes and consequences. You need to think about how you express the links between **causes** and **effects**.

Learning outcomes

By the end of this lesson, you will understand how to:

- use conjunctions to link and indicate the relationship between points
- use non-finite verbs to link relevant information or indicate the relationship between points.

Definitions

Co-ordinating conjunction: a word used to link two clauses of equal importance within a sentence, e.g. 'and', 'but', 'so', 'or', etc.

Subordinate clause: a clause that adds detail to or develops the main clause, linked with a subordinating conjunction such as 'because', 'when', 'if', 'although', etc.

How can I link my points in sentences to show cause and effect?

When explaining complex sequences of events, use co-ordinating conjunctions to link them in sentences. Look at this exam-style narrative analysis task:

> Write a narrative account analysing the key events of the Soviet invasion of Afghanistan. **(8 marks)**

1. How could you link these three points using just co-ordinating conjunctions, e.g. 'and', 'but', 'so'?

> In 1978 the pro-Soviet government in Afghanistan was toppled in a local coup.
>
> The Soviet Union learned that the new government was in talks with the USA.
>
> The Soviet Union was worried about losing influence in the region and invaded Afghanistan in December 1979.

2. You can also use subordinating conjunctions to make the relationship between cause and effect clear. For example, linking:

- an explanation: (e.g. 'because', 'as', 'in order that', etc)
- a condition: (e.g. 'if', 'unless', etc)
- a comparison: (e.g. 'although', 'whereas', 'despite', etc)
- a sequence: (e.g. 'when', 'as', 'before', 'after', 'until', etc).

Look at these simple, short questions and answers:

a. Why did the Soviet Union want a pro-Soviet government in Afghanistan? *It did not want hardline Muslim ideology to spread from Iran to the Soviet Union.*

b. What made the Soviet Union concerned about Hafizullah Amin and his government? *He was in talks with the USA.*

c. What reason did the Soviet Union give for invading Afghanistan? *They said they had been invited by Amin to help him deal with terrorism.*

d. What happened after Hafizullah Amin was killed? *He was replaced by the pro-Soviet Babrak Kamal.*

Rewrite the information in each question and answer as a single sentence. Choose a different type of subordinating conjunction (explanation, condition, comparison and sequence) in each one to express the relationship between cause and effect as clearly as possible.

3. Experiment with different ways of using a subordinating conjunction to link two or more of your sentences into a single sentence.

How can I link my points in other ways?

You can add relevant information and further explanation of cause and effect using non-finite verbs. These include facing / faced, determining / determined, cutting / cut.

Compare these two extracts, written in response to the exam-style question on the previous page.

> The Soviet Union became concerned that it would lose influence in Afghanistan because it learned that Hafizullah Amin was in talks with the USA.

Two points are linked using a subordinating conjunction.

> Learning that Hafizullah Amin was in talks with the USA, the Soviet Union became concerned that it would lose influence in Afghanistan.

Two points are linked using a non-finite verb.

Look at the two sentences below. How could you link the two points in each one, using a non-finite verb instead of a conjunction? **Hint:** think about how you could use a non-finite form of the highlighted verb.

> President Carter claimed that the invasion was a major threat to world peace, so he increased spending on arms.

> President Carter announced the 'Carter Doctrine' in January 1980, and soon after imposed economic sanctions on the Soviet Union.

Did you notice?

There are lots of different ways to link points in sentences. Some of them make the relationship between points more clearly than others.

4. Choose **one** of the sentences above. Experiment with rewriting it in two or three different ways, using different methods to link points. Which version expresses the relationship most clearly and fluently?

Improving an answer

Now look at this paragraph from the beginning of one student's response to the narrative analysis task on the previous page.

> In 1978 the pro-Soviet government in Afghanistan was toppled in a coup. In the following year there was a revolution in Iran. This brought in a new Muslim fundamentalist government. This worried the Soviets. They did not want fundamentalist ideas spreading to the Muslim population in the Soviet Union. They were also worried about losing influence in Afghanistan when the new ruler Hafizullah Amin held talks with the US government.

5. Try rewriting this paragraph, using conjunctions and non-finite verbs to make the sequence of events, and the relationship between cause and effect, clear.

6. Continue the response above with a second paragraph explaining how the situation developed. Use conjunctions and non-finite verbs to make clear connections between causes and effects.

The difference between a story and a narrative account that analyses

Paper 2, Question 2 will ask you to 'Write a narrative account analysing … .' (see page 95 in *Preparing for your exams*). You are not being asked to tell a story in the examination; you are being asked to explain how events led to an outcome. This means showing that the events are a series of happenings that have links between them. To do this, you must show that:

- events are prompted by something
- these events react with other events (or perhaps they react with existing circumstances)
- consequences follow from them.

Showing links like these is what turns a story into 'an account that analyses'.

Narratives for young children are always stories; they deal with events and descriptions. For example, many versions of the adventures of Toad of Toad Hall, originally described in the children's book *The Wind in the Willows*, have been published. These narratives show how Toad got himself into a number of scrapes. One episode describes his fixation with acquiring a fast car, his theft of one, his arrest for dangerous driving and his subsequent trial and imprisonment.

Here are some extracts from *The Wind in the Willows*.

Toad steals a motor car

Toad had a passion for cars. He saw a car in the middle of the yard, quite unattended. Toad walked slowly round it. 'I wonder,' he said to himself, 'if this car starts easily.' Next moment he was turning the starting handle. Then he heard the sound of the engine and, as if in a dream, he found himself in the driver's seat. He drove the car out through the archway and the car leapt forward through the open country…

This extract has the first important ingredient of narrative: sequence – putting events in the right order. Words and phrases like 'next moment' and 'then' show the sequence. However, it lacks the analytical links between events. In this case, key links could be built around phrases such as 'because', 'in order to' or 'as a result of this'.

For example:

Toad saw the car parked in the middle of the yard. Because there was no one with it, he took the opportunity to have a good look at it. He even gave the starting handle a turn in order to see how easily it started. It started easily, but the sound of the engine affected Toad so much that his old passion for cars resurfaced and his urge to drive the car increased to such an extent that it became irresistible. As a result, as if in a dream, he found himself in the driver's seat…

The analytical narrative, as well as linking events, also makes clear what followed on from them – what difference they made. It uses process words and phrases that show something was happening. In this example, the process words and phrases are 'affected', 'resurfaced', 'increased' and 'became'.

Activities ?

1. Choose a story that you know well – or think of a plot for a story of your own.

2. Select up to eight key events in the story and list them in a sequence. Ideally, these events should be from the beginning, middle and end of the story (if two things happen at the same time you can list them together). Create a flow chart with arrows from one event to the next in the sequence. Label your arrows with links chosen from the chain of linkages (see Figure 1).

3. Write a narrative account analysing the key events of your story. Use the links and at least five process words. Choose them from the process word case (see Figure 2) or use others of your own. Remember that events can combine with long-standing feelings or circumstances as part of the narrative (for example, Toad's passion for motorcars).

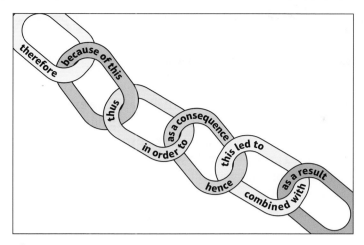

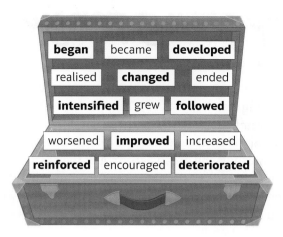

Figure 1 The chain of linkages

Figure 2 Process word case

Writing historical accounts analysing...

You may be asked to write an account that analyses the key events which led to something, or the key events of a crisis, or the way in which something developed. This example has shown the skills you will need to write a good historical account. As you prepare for your examination, you should practise by:

- selecting key events
- sequencing them
- linking them into a process that explains an outcome.

As you study the events of the Cold War, note the linking phrases and process words the author has used in this book. You should add them to your own lists. When you create your own analytical historical narratives, try to make use of both linking phrases and process vocabulary.

Activities ?

Study the timeline on page 20. You can use the events from it to help you to answer the following question:

Write a narrative account analysing the development of Europe into two blocs in the years 1947–49

1 With a partner, write the events on pieces of card, without their dates, and then:

   a practise sequencing them correctly

   b agree on another one or two events you could choose to include in your account and any events you could remove

   c identify an instance where long-standing circumstances (or attitudes) were involved as events unfolded.

2 Working individually, write your own narrative account, with linkages and showing a process. Focus on what it is you are explaining and choose process words which relate to, e.g. the setting up of different organisations and alliances.

3 Either swap accounts with a partner or check your own account. Highlight linkages in yellow and process words in green. You can use the same words more than once, but aim to have at least five green and five yellow highlights. See if using more 'process words' improves your account even more.

You are now ready to complete your exam question. Remember to use **SSLaP**.

- **S**elect key events and developments.
- **S**equence them in the right order.
- **L**ink them, **a**nd

- Show the **P**rocess that led to the outcome of your analytical narrative.

Preparing for your GCSE Paper 2 exam

Paper 2 overview

Your Paper 2 is in two sections that examine the Period Study and British Depth Study. They each count for 20% of your History assessment. The questions on Superpower relations and the Cold War (1941–91) are the Period Study and are in Section A of the exam paper. You should use just under half the time allowed for Paper 2 to write your answers to Section A. This will give you a few moments for checking your answers at the end of Section B.

History Paper 2	Period Study and British Depth Study			Time 1 hour 45 mins
Section A	Period Study	Answer 3 questions	32 marks	50 minutes
Section B	Depth Options B1 or B2	Answer 3 questions	32 marks	55 minutes

Period Study Option 26 / 27: Superpower relations and the Cold War, 1941–91

You will answer Questions 1, 2 and 3.

1 Explain two consequences of... (2 x 4 marks)

Allow ten minutes to write your answer. Write about each consequence. You are given just over half a page for each. Use this as a guide for answer length. You should keep the answer brief and not try to add more information on extra lines. This will make sure you allow enough time for later questions worth more marks. Make sure you focus on consequence: *as a result; as a consequence; the effect was* are useful phrases to use.

2 Write a narrative account analysing... (8 marks)

This question asks you to write a narrative explaining how events led to an outcome. Allow 15 minutes to write your answer. You are given two information points as prompts to help you. You do not have to use the prompts and you will not lose marks by leaving them out. Always remember to add in a new point of your own as well. Higher marks are gained by adding in a point extra to the prompts. You will be given at least two pages of lines in the answer booklet for your answer. This does not mean you should try to fill all the space. The front page of the exam paper tells you 'there may be more space than you need'. Aim to write an organised answer, putting events in the right order and showing how one connected to the next. Your narrative should have a clear beginning, middle and end.

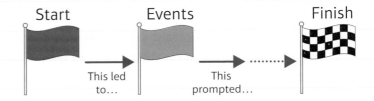

3 Explain two of the following... (2 x 8 marks)

This question is worth half your marks for the whole Period Study. Make sure you have kept 25 minutes of the exam time to answer. It asks you to explain the importance of events and developments. You have a choice of two out of three. Take time to make the choice. Before you decide, be clear what you have to explain: the question is always worded as 'The importance of... for... .' It is a good idea during revision to practise identifying the importance of key events **for** something: what did they affect or lead to? Ask yourself: 'What difference did they make to it?' or 'Why did they matter?' Be clear about your reasons for saying something is important.

Paper 2, Question 1

Explain **two** consequences of the decisions made by The Grand Alliance at the Yalta Conference in February 1945. **(8 marks)**

Average answer

Consequence 1:
As a result of the Yalta Conference, Germany was divided into different zones. There were four of these governed by different countries. This division led to a lot of difficulties in the future.

> This answer has identified a consequence and given a brief description. However, it needs more detail to provide an effective explanation

Consequence 2:
Another consequence of the conference was that there was disagreement about how Poland was to be governed. It was agreed that there would be a government decided by free elections, but there was disagreement about who The Grand Alliance wanted to win those elections. This led to further tension.

> This needs more examples and explanation. The second sentence does not explain fully how the decision led to disagreements between different members of The Grand Alliance.

Verdict

This is an average answer because it identifies two consequences with some support, but it needs more explanation of consequence with specific information. Use the feedback to rewrite this answer, making as many improvements as you can.

Paper 2, Question 1

Explain **two** consequences of the decisions made by The Grand Alliance at the Yalta Conference in February 1945. **(8 marks)**

Exam tip

The question wants you to explain the results of something. What difference did it make? Use phrases such as 'as a result' or 'the effect of this was'.

Strong answer

Consequence 1:
At the Yalta Conference the Big Three decided what would happen to Germany after the war. As a result of the conference Germany was divided into four zones, controlled by Britain, the USA, the Soviet Union and France. Each country had the right to govern its sector as it saw fit. However, Stalin believed that in the end he had been given the poorest sector and resented the fact that the Western Allies administered the wealthier parts. So this led to worse relations between East and West as Germany became an area of tension.

A clear explanation of the impact of the division of Germany, with specific factual support.

Consequence 2:
Yalta led to an increase in suspicion between Stalin and the USA / Britain. This suspicion was as a result of the failure to agree on how Poland should be governed. There was general agreement that a government would be elected using free elections, but this meant different things to each country. To Stalin it meant using his influence to ensure a pro-Moscow government. Britain and the USA supported the 'London Poles' who were non-Communists. Stalin wanted a Communist government in Poland as part of his plan to build a buffer zone. He saw the action of Britain and the USA as trying to undermine the security of the Soviet Union. So relations worsened.

A valid point very well explained, with a high level of factual support.

Verdict

This is a strong answer because it has explained two consequences and supported both with specific information showing good knowledge of the period.

Paper 2, Question 2

Write a narrative account analysing the key events leading to the break-up of the Warsaw Pact in the years 1985–91. You may use the following in your answer:

- Gorbachev became leader of the Soviet Union in 1985
- the fall of the Berlin Wall in 1989.

You **must** also use information of your own. **(8 marks)**

Exam tip

Remember that the key to scoring well on this type of question is to explain how one event leads to the next in a logical and structured way.

Average answer

When Gorbachev came to power in the Soviet Union he had a new way of thinking. He abandoned the Brezhnev Doctrine and had more open government in the Soviet Union. This loosening of the grip was noticed in the Soviet satellite countries and they began to break away from the control of the Soviet Union. First of all, East Germans started leaving for the West through Hungary. Then Poland had free elections and the communists lost. In October the Berlin Wall came down and in the next month there was a revolution in Czechoslovakia. In July 1991 the Warsaw Pact was dissolved.

This answer has listed the main events but it does not show the links in the 'developing story'.

Verdict

This is an average answer because, whilst it shows an understanding of the events, they are not clearly linked together to show a coherent narrative. Use the feedback to rewrite this answer, making as many improvements as you can.

Paper 2, Question 2

Write a narrative account analysing the key events
leading to the break-up of the Warsaw Pact in the years 1985–91.
You may use the following in your answer:

- Gorbachev became leader of the Soviet Union in 1985
- the fall of the Berlin Wall in 1989.

You **must** also use information of your own. **(8 marks)**

Strong answer

The break-up of the Warsaw Pact probably started when Gorbachev came
to power in the Soviet Union. Although he did not intend to end Soviet
domination of Eastern Europe, Gorbachev decided that the Soviet Union
could not continue to spend huge sums on the arms race and foreign policy.
Because of this, in 1985 he announced that the Soviet Union was abandoning
the Brezhnev Doctrine.

As a result, the members of the Warsaw Pact realised they could now
introduce reforms in their countries, without fear of being invaded by
Warsaw Pact forces like Hungary and Czechoslovakia were many years
earlier. So when, in September 1989, East Germans started travelling to West
Germany through Hungary and Austria little was done to stop them. The
countries of Eastern and Western Europe were becoming more connected.
In the same month, the communist government in Poland was replaced after
earlier being defeated in free elections. In October, communist government
came to an end in Hungary. Moscow made no attempt to prevent the Polish
elections or get rid of the new non-communist leaders in either country.
Since the Warsaw Pact existed mainly to protect its communist members
from the West, the reasons for its existence were fading away.

> This paragraph follows
> on neatly from the one
> before, explaining a link
> between events in the
> Soviet Union and events
> in Warsaw Pact countries.

The fall of the Berlin Wall in 1989 made it even clearer that East and West
were not divided any more. Its fall was symbolic and encouraged further
challenges to communist rule. Communist regimes in Czechoslovakia and
Romania were also toppled shortly afterwards. By the summer of 1990 all
the old communist governments of the satellite states were replaced by new
governments that had been democratically elected. With most countries of
Eastern Europe now being led by non-communist governments there was no
need for the Warsaw Pact. As a result, it was dissolved in July 1991.

> This paragraph makes a
> clear link between events
> and the implications for
> the Warsaw Pact.

Verdict

This is a strong answer because it organises the events described in a
coherent sequence, highlighting the links between them, and relates
them to the break-up of the Warsaw Pact.

Paper 2, Question 3

Explain **two** of the following:

* The importance of the Truman Doctrine for international relations after the Second World War
* The importance of the building of the Berlin Wall for the development of the Cold War
* The importance of the Olympic boycotts for relations between the USA and the Soviet Union. **(16 marks)**

The sample answer below covers just the bullet point about the Olympic boycotts. Don't forget in the exam you need to write about two.

Exam tip

The question asks about importance but each bullet point also gives you a 'for' – e.g. 'for the development of the Cold War'. Don't just tell the story of the event – e.g. the building of the Berlin Wall. Make sure you also explain the impact. How did it change things **for** the development of the Cold War?

Average answer

The Olympic boycotts were very important. At this time relations between the USA and the Soviet Union were getting worse. They became even worse when the Soviet Union invaded Afghanistan. So the Americans wanted a way to punish the Soviet Union. They did this by persuading lots of countries not to attend the Moscow Olympics in 1980. That really upset the Soviet Union because it was hoping to use the Olympics to show everyone how great communism was and how successful athletes from Warsaw Pact countries were (so proving that communist society was better).

The Soviet Union was really upset about the boycott and got its revenge four years later when it led a boycott of the Olympics being held in Los Angeles. So the Cold War got colder.

This answer has correctly identified that the boycotts were important in intensifying the Cold War and explained why the boycott upset the Soviet Union.

The writer uses 'really upset' twice. It would be better to go into more depth about how the Soviet Union reacted.

Verdict

This is an average answer because it does not provide enough explanation of what the impact of the boycotts was. It is also short on specific information to support the answer. Use the feedback to rewrite this answer, making as many improvements as you can.

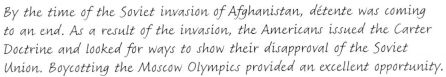

Explain **two** of the following:

- The importance of the Truman Doctrine for international relations after the Second World War
- The importance of the building of the Berlin Wall for the development of the Cold War
- The importance of the Olympic boycotts for relations between the USA and the Soviet Union. **(16 marks)**

> The sample answer below covers just the bullet point about the Olympic boycotts. Don't forget in the exam you need to write about two.

Strong answer

By the time of the Soviet invasion of Afghanistan, détente was coming to an end. As a result of the invasion, the Americans issued the Carter Doctrine and looked for ways to show their disapproval of the Soviet Union. Boycotting the Moscow Olympics provided an excellent opportunity.

This really upset the Soviet Union because it was hoping to use the Olympics to show everyone how great communism was and how successful athletes from Warsaw Pact countries were (so proving that communist society was better). So the American boycott was important because it made it plain to the Soviet Union that the period of co-operation was over and that the USA still considered itself as the leader of the democratic world, ready to resist attempts to spread communism.

> This answer correctly identifies that the boycotts were important in intensifying the Cold War.

Equally, the Moscow boycott angered the Soviet Union which retaliated by leading the Warsaw Pact countries in a boycott of the Los Angeles Olympics in 1984. This showed the world was still divided in two camps, East and West.

So the Olympic boycotts made the Cold War colder and showed that the USA and the Soviet Union were still bitter rivals.

> There is also factual support to explain how the boycotts intensified the Cold War.

Verdict

This is a strong answer because it explains importance by showing the consequences of the boycotts and their impact on the Cold War. It supports the argument with good detail.

Answers to Recall Quiz questions

Chapter 1

1 Soviet Union, USA, Britain
2 Tehran – 1943, Yalta – 1945, Potsdam – 1945
3 Stalin, Roosevelt, Churchill, then: Stalin, Truman, Attlee
4 Truman said the spread of communism should be stopped and the USA would help countries that did not want to become communist
5 A state that is under the control of another state. Satellite states in Eastern Europe were controlled by the Soviet Union
6 Britain, France, USA and nine others
7 Soviet Union, Poland, Czechoslovakia, Hungary, Romania, Bulgaria, Albania, East Germany
8 1949
9 Inter-continental ballistic missile
10 Khrushchev

Chapter 2

1 Because Germany was occupied by the Soviets from the East and the democratic allies from the West. The country was divided into zones and so was the capital, Berlin
2 Large numbers of educated people were leaving East Germany for the West
3 Eisenhower, Kennedy, Johnson, Nixon
4 Khrushchev, Brezhnev
5 To show support for the people of West Berlin
6 1959
7 An attempt to topple Castro's government using CIA-trained Cuban exiles
8 Test Ban Treaty (1963), Outer Space Treaty (1967), Nuclear Non-Proliferation Treaty (1968)
9 The spring of 1968, when Alexander Dubcek tried to reform communism in Czechoslovakia
10 He first warned Dubcek to reverse the reforms, then sent Warsaw Pact troops to re-establish Soviet control

Chapter 3

1 1975
2 The invasion of Afghanistan by the Soviet Union
3 The Soviet Union led a boycott of the 1984 Los Angeles Olympics
4 Poland
5 Strategic Defense Initiative – a plan to place satellites in orbit that could shoot down nuclear missiles fired at the USA
6 Brezhnev, Andropov, Chernenko, Gorbachev
7 The USA and Soviet Union would abolish all land-based missiles with a range of 500–5,500 km
8 The Berlin Wall came down
9 Boris Yeltsin
10 25 December 1991

Index

Key terms are capitalised initially, in bold type with an asterisk.
Entry headings for topic booklets are shown in italics.

Acknowledgements

With thanks to Paulette Catherwood for additional authoring support

Picture Credits

The publisher would like to thank the following for their kind permission to reproduce their photographs:

(Key: b-bottom; c-centre; l-left; r-right; t-top)

akg-images Ltd: ullstein bild 75; **Alamy Images:** CTK 17, Everett Collection Historical 26, Keystone Pictures USA 47, The Art Archive 3tl, The Illustrated London News Picture Library. Ingram Publishing 10c, 13; **Bridgeman Art Library Ltd:** 78; **Corbis:** Bettmann 8, 30, 31, Hulton-Deutsch / Hulton-Deutsch Collection 21, Hulton-Deutsch Collection 7b; **Getty Images:** Bettmann 40, 43, 46, 52, 68, 50B, 50T, DIANE-LU HOVASSE / AFP 85, Dirck Halstead / The LIFE Images Collection 7t, 70, Hulton Archive / Stringer 10t, 34, Keystone-France / Gamma-Keystone 59, Lehnartz / ullstein bild 45, Universal History Archive / UIG 83, UniversalImagesGroup 10b; **Mary Evans Picture Library:** picture-alliance / dpa 66, 84; **Mirrorpix:** 15; **NASA:** S75-22410 71; **The Herb Block Foundation:** A 1962 Herblock Cartoon 56

Cover images: *Front:* **Getty Images:** Grey Villet / The LIFE Images Collection

All other images © Pearson Education

We are grateful to the following for permission to reproduce copyright material:

Text

Extract in Source D on page 16 from Telegram from Nikolai Novikov, Soviet Ambassador to the US, to the Soviet Leadership 27/09/46, History and Public Policy Program Digital Archive, AVP SSSR, f. 06. op. 8, p. 45, p. 759, History and Public Policy Program Digital Archive, with permission from the Cold War International History Project; Extract in Source E on page 16 from Winston Churchill The Sinews of Peace ("Iron Curtain Speech") 05/03/1946 reproduced with permission of Curtis Brown, London on behalf of the Estate of Winston S. Churchill, Copyright © The Estate of Winston S. Churchill; Quote on page 22 from Ernest Bevin from a statement made at a National Press Club lunch in Washington, 01/04/49 Harry S. Truman Library; Extract in Source C on page 22 from the "Marshall Plan" speech at Harvard University, 05/06/47, Courtesy of the George C. Marshall Foundation, Lexington, Virginia; Extract in Source F on page 27 from The North Atlantic Treaty Washington D.C. 04/04/49, NATO; Quote on page 33 from *Khrushchev: And the First Russian Spring*, Charles Scribner's Sons (Fyodor M. Burlatsky), Orion Publishing Group Ltd with permission; Extract in Interpretation 1 on page 44 from Milestones: 1953–1960/U-2 Overflights and the Capture of Francis Gary Powers, 1960, Office of the Historian, U.S. State Department; Extract in Source D on page 44 from Radio and Television Report to the American People on the Berlin Crisis, July 25, 1961, John F. Kennedy; Quote on page 47 from Remarks at the Rudolph Wilde Platz, Berlin, John F Kennedy, 26/06/63, Extract in Source G on page 47 from John F Kennedy – Remarks at the Rudolph Wilde Platz, Berlin 26/06/1963; Extract in Source C, page 51, quote on page 52, extract in Source E on page 53 from Selected Foreign Policy Documents from the Administration of John F. Kennedy Jan 1961–Nov 1963: London, the Stationery Office 2001, Military Resources: Bay of Pigs Invasion & Cuban Missile Crisis, The U.S. National Archives and Records Administration; Quote on page 55 from John Foster Dulles, interview in Time-Life Magazine Time-Life Volume 40, No 3 16/01/1956 p.78, with permission from The Reader's Digest Magazine UK; Extract in Source F on page 55 from Khrushchev Remembers: The Last Testament by Nikita Khrushchev, translated and edited by Strobe Talbott. Copyright © 1974 by Little, Brown and Company (Inc). Used by permission of Little, Brown and Company; Extract in Source D on page 60 from *Pravda, September 25, 1968*, Vol. 7, No. 6 (November 1968), pp. 1323–1325 International Legal Materials, reproduced with permission of American Society of International Law, in the format Republish in a book via Copyright Clearance Center; Extract in Source D on page 71 from The Helsinki Accords, US President Gerald Ford; Extract in Source C on page 78 from *An American Life*, Reprint edition ed., Threshold Editions (Reagan, R) p.266, Copyright © 1990 Ronald W. Reagan reprinted with the permission of Simon & Schuster, Inc. and Janklow & Nesbit Associates. All rights reserved; Extract in Source E on page 84 from Fall of the Berlin wall – 25 years on: 'We were always aware that another part of Berlin existed', *Independent*, 31/10/2014 (Robert Vielhaber).